Cells

Cell components 4.1.1.2

Animal and plant cells share some, but not all organelles.

Plant cell

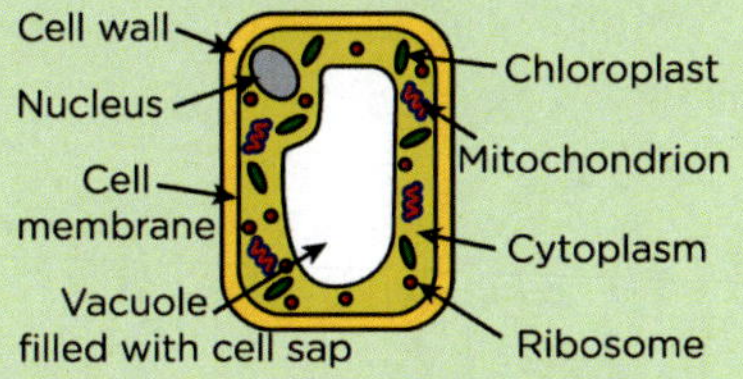

Animal cell

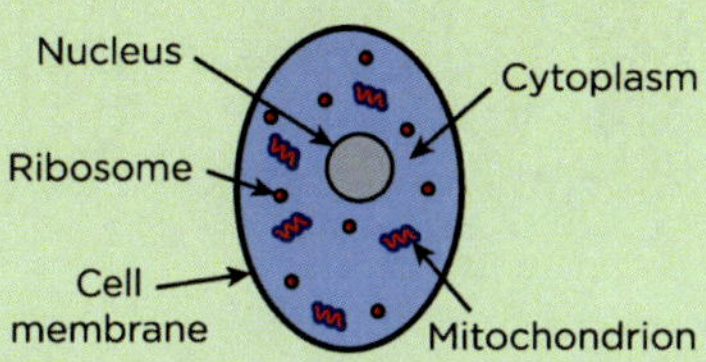

- Mitochondria are the site of aerobic respiration where energy is released from glucose.
- Cytoplasm is water-based and contains lots of the organelles. It is where most cell reactions take place.
- Nucleus contains deoxyribonucleic acid (DNA), which is the genetic information that controls the cell. DNA is organised into chromosomes.
- Cell membrane encloses the cell and controls which substances go in and out. Many simple substances travel by diffusion.
- Ribosomes are the site of protein synthesis.
- Chloroplasts (plant cells) contain the green pigment chlorophyll, which absorbs light for photosynthesis.
- Cell wall (plant and algal cells) made of cellulose, which strengthens the cell.

Bacterial cell

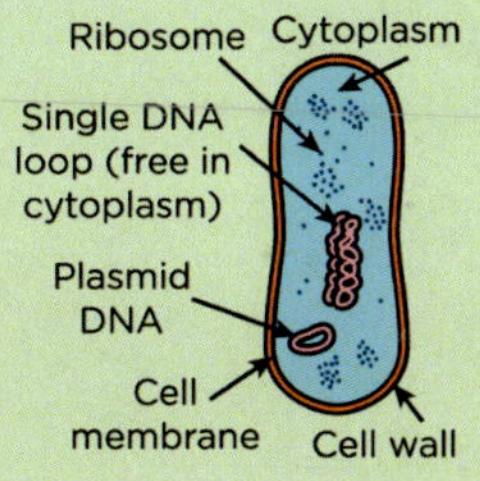

Eukaryotes and prokaryotes 4.1.1.1

Eukaryotic cells	Prokaryotic cells
Plant and animal cells	Bacterial cells
Cell membrane	Cell membrane surrounded by a cell wall
Cytoplasm	Cytoplasm
Genetic material enclosed in a nucleus	Genetic material is a single DNA loop and sometimes small rings of DNA called plasmids, not enclosed in a nucleus.
Larger (5 µm – 100 µm)	Smaller (1 µm – 10 µm)

10^{-9} nano (n) → (x 1000) → 10^{-6} micro (µ) → (x 1000) → 10^{-3} milli (m) → (x 10) → 10^{-2} centi (c)

Cell differentiation 4.1.1.4

- Cell differentiation is the specialisation of cells by acquiring different sub-cellular structures. This is required so cells can perform their specific functions.
- Cells differentiate to form different types of cells:
  - Most animal cells differentiate at an early stage. In mature animals, cell division is restricted to repairing and replacing damaged and old cells.
  - Many plant cells can differentiate throughout life.

Ce… s

- Cells may have a speci… function:

Cell		
Sperm cell (animal) 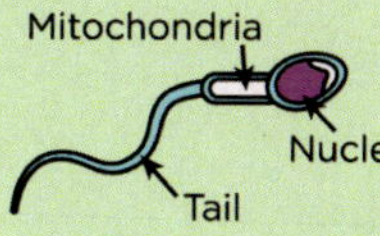	… female reproductive system towards an ovum (egg cell) to fertilise it	• Tail to swim • Large number of mitochondria to release energy to swim
Nerve cell (animal) 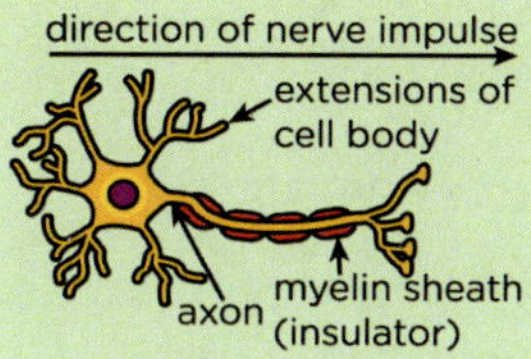	Transmit electrical signals quickly through nervous system	• Long cell extension (axons) • Myelin sheath insulator increases the speed of transmission of electrical impulses • Cell body has extensions to pick up signals from neighbouring cells
Muscle cell (animal) 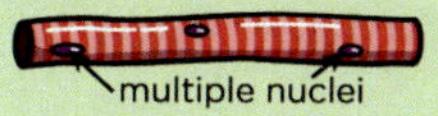	Contract and relax	• Large number of mitochondria to provide energy for contraction
Root hair cell (plant) 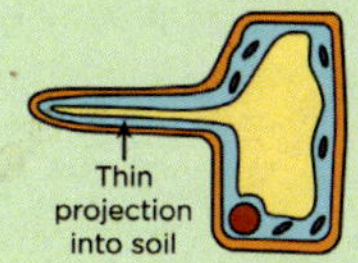	Absorb water and minerals from soil	• Small thin extension to increase surface area for absorption of water and minerals
Xylem (plant) 	Carry water and dissolved minerals upwards from roots up plant stems for transpiration	• Empty dead cells form long hollow tubes with no end walls • Lignin inside walls supports plant weight
Phloem cell (plant) 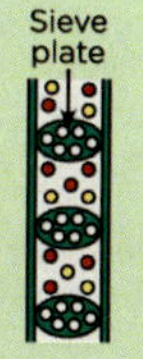	Carry sucrose in cell sap from leaves to other parts of the plant via translocation	• Living cells form tubes • Contain few organelles so sugar travels easily • End walls contain small holes (sieve plates)

Microscopy, cultures, mitosis, and human stem cells

SNAPREVI

Microscopy 4.1.1.5

- Light microscopes were invented first, with a maximum resolution of 200nm.
  - Eyepiece lens often has x10 magnification.
  - Often 3 objective lenses of different magnifications (x5, x10, and x25).
  - Stage holds the specimen.
  - Specimen is on a microscope slide under a cover slip.
  - Course focus quickly moves the stage closer and further from the chosen objective lens to roughly focus the sample.
  - Fine focus moves the stage slowly to finely focus the sample.

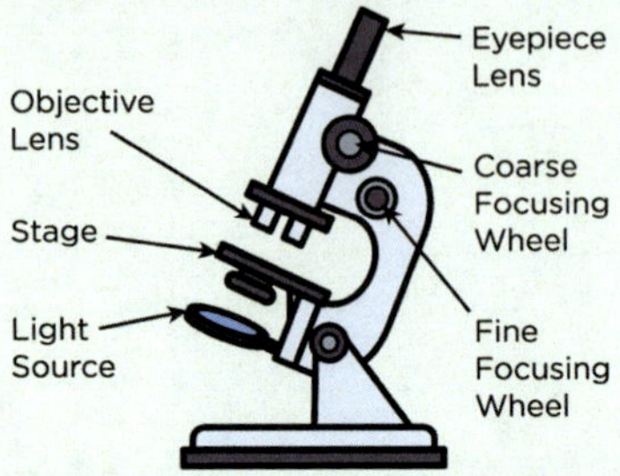

- Electron microscopes were invented later, with an increased maximum resolution of 0.1nm.
  - Transmission electron microscope (TEM) fires a beam of electrons through a thin slice of the specimen. Electrons that pass through the specimen are detected and used to make the image.
  - Scanning electron microscope (SEM) fires a beam of electrons across the surface of the specimen. Electrons scatter from the surface and are detected to make the image.
- Electron microscopes have a higher magnification and resolving power than light microscopes, increasing the understanding of sub-cellular structures.
- $\boldsymbol{magnification = \frac{size\ of\ image}{size\ of\ real\ object}}$

Human stem cells 4.1.2.3

- A stem cell is an undifferentiated cell capable of replication and differentiation into other types of cell.
- In human embryos, embryonic stem cells can differentiate into any type of specialised human cell (totipotent). Once it has differentiated, it cannot change back or switch cell type.
- In adult bone marrow, adult stem cells can form many specific cell types, such as blood stem cells producing blood cells (multipotent).
- Human stem cells can be used in therapeutic cloning to help conditions such as diabetes and paralysis.
  - An embryo is produced with the same genes as the patient.
  - Stem cells from the embryo are not rejected by the patient's body.
  - Potential risks include transfer of viral infection and some people have ethical or religious objections.

Culturing microorganisms 4.1.1.6

- Bacteria multiply by cell division (binary fission) as frequently as once every 20 minutes.
- Bacteria only multiply if they have enough nutrients and a suitable temperature.
  - Bacteria can be grown in a nutrient broth solution.
  - Bacteria can be grown as colonies on an agar gel plate.
- Uncontaminated cultures of microorganisms are used to investigate the action of disinfectants and antibiotics. They are prepared using aseptic technique:
  - Petri dishes and culture media must be sterilised before use to prevent growing foreign microorganisms.
  - Inoculating loops must be sterilised by passing them through a flame before being used to transfer microorganisms to the petri dish.
  - The Petri dish should be stored upside down with the lid secured with adhesive tape to reduce the contamination risk from airborne microorganisms and stop condensation from pooling.
  - Cultures should be incubated at 25 °C to encourage growth of the microorganisms without growing contaminating microorganisms from humans (which grow best at 37 °C).
- $\boldsymbol{bacteria\ in\ population = initial\ total \times 2^{number\ of\ divisions}}$
- $\boldsymbol{area\ of colony/clear\ area = \pi r^2}$

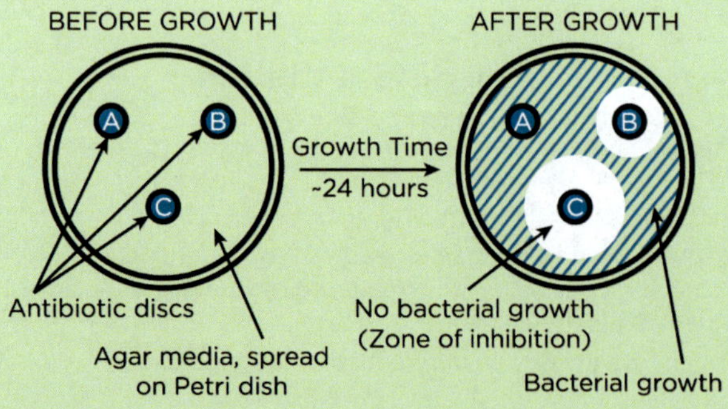

Effect of three antibiotics (A, B and C) on bacterial growth.

- A = No effect
- B = Inhibits growth weakly
- C = Inhibits growth strongly

Chromosomes 4.1.

- Chromosomes are found in the nucleus. They are made up of DNA with each chromosome carrying a large number of genes.
- Chromosomes are usually found in pairs in body cells.
- Gene = section of DNA that codes for a specific protein.
- Alleles = Different versions of the same gene.

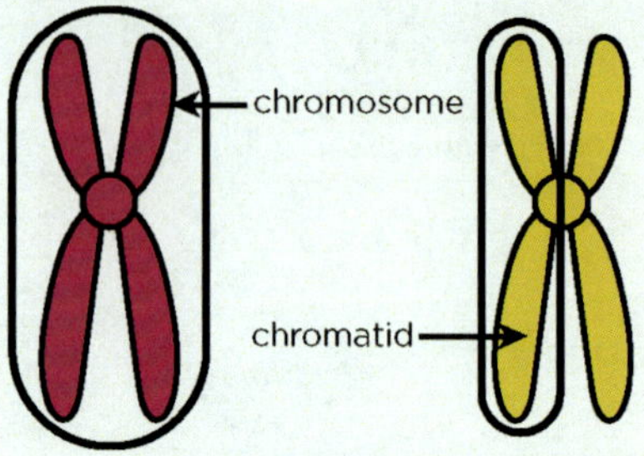

Mitosis 4.1.2

- Cells divide in a series of stages called the cell cycle.
  - Stage 1 – Interphase: cell growth, increase in number of organelles, DNA replicates so there are 2 copies of each chromosome (diploid).
  - Stage 2 – Mitosis: one set of chromosomes is pulled to each end of the cell and the nucleus divides.
  - Stage 3 – Cytokinesis: cytoplasm and cell membrane divide to form 2 identical daughter cells.
- Mitosis is important in the growth and development of multicellular organisms. It also replaces old or damaged cells.

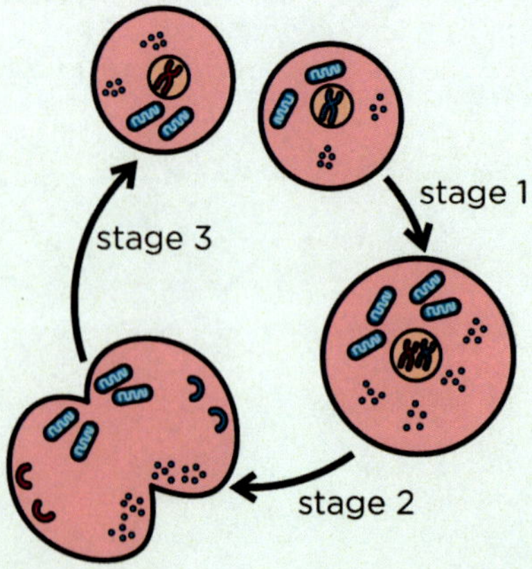

lant stem cells, diffusion, and osmosis

Diffusion 4.1.3.1

Diffusion is the net movement of particles in solution or of a gas from an area of higher concentration to an area of lower concentration.

Examples include:

- Oxygen and carbon dioxide in gas exchange.
- Waste urea from cells into the blood plasma for excretion in the kidney.

Factors affecting diffusion rate:

- Steeper concentration gradients increase diffusion rate.
- Higher temperatures increase diffusion rate
- Increasing surface area increases diffusion rate.

Diffusion in humans 4.1.3.1

The effectiveness of exchange surfaces is increased by having:

- A large surface area
- A thin membrane (short distance for diffusion)
- Efficient blood supply in animals
- Well-ventilated in animals for gas exchange
- Moist membrane in animals for gas exchange

Small intestine

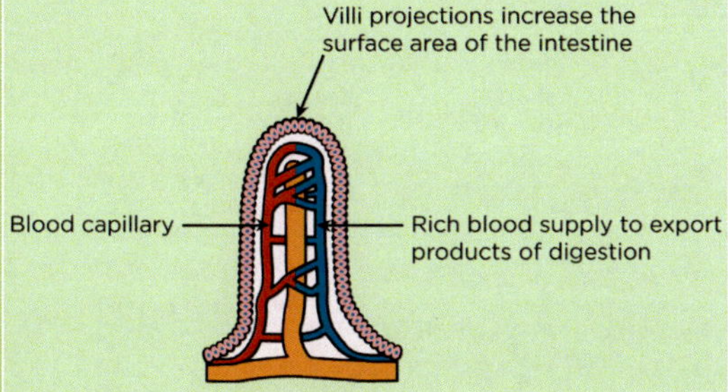

Lungs

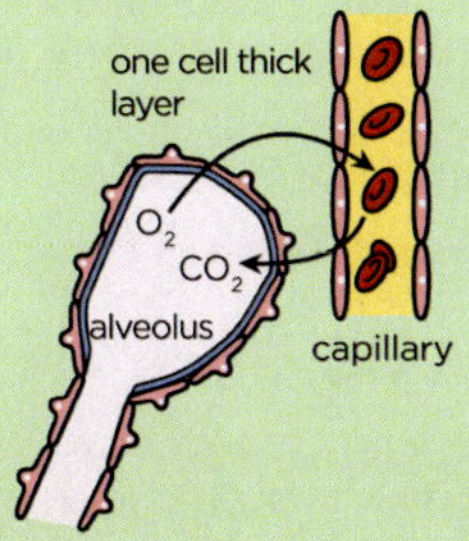

Diffusion in other organisms 4.1.3.1

Gills

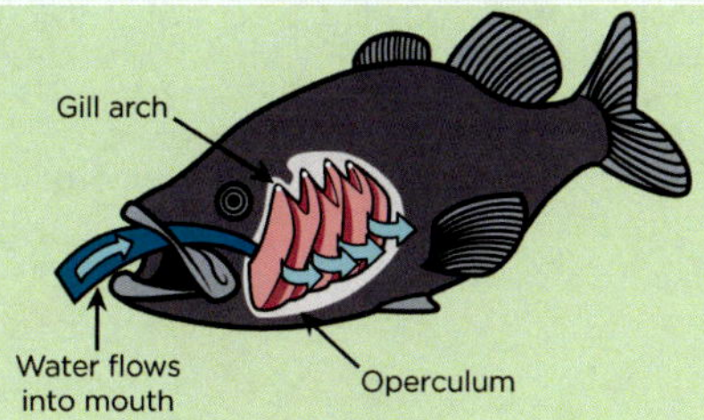

Roots

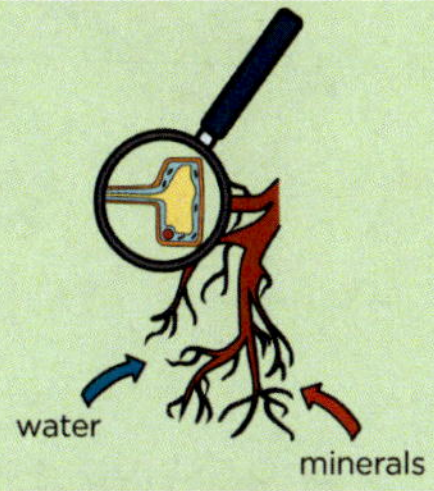

Leaves

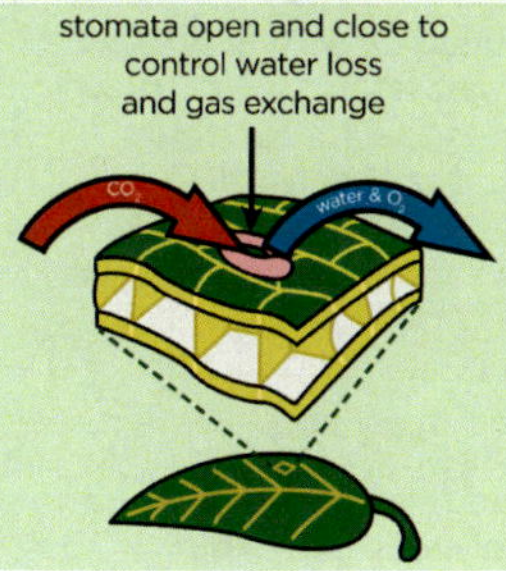

Surface area to volume ratio 4.1.3.1

- A large surface area to volume ratio increases the rate of diffusion.
- To calculate surface area to volume ratio, divide the surface area by the volume.
  - $\boldsymbol{Surface\ area\ of\ cube = 6\ sides \times length^2}$
  - $\boldsymbol{Volume\ of\ cube = length^3}$
- Single-celled organisms have a large surface area to volume ratio so molecules can move into and out of the cell to meet the needs of the organism.
- Multicellular organisms have a small surface area to volume ratio so require an exchange surface and transport system to sufficiently move substances around the organism.

Osmosis 4.1.3.2

- Osmosis is the diffusion of water from a dilute solution to a concentrated solution through a partially permeable membrane, such as the cell membrane.
- Cells can be placed in solutions with different relative concentrations.
  - Isotonic = concentration inside the cell is the same as the concentration of the solution. No net movement of water.
  - Hypertonic = concentration of the solution is higher than the concentration inside the cell.
  - Hypotonic = concentration of the solution is lower than the concentration inside the cell.

Solution	Animal cell	Plant cell
Hypertonic (e.g. salty brine)	Shrunken/shrivelled 	Flaccid → plasmolysed 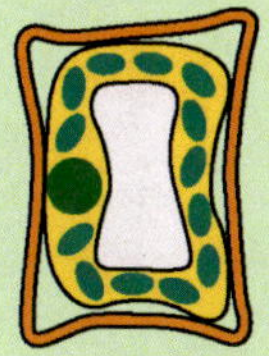
Hypotonic (e.g. pure water)	Swell and burst 	Turgid 

- $Percentage\ change = \frac{final\ value - initial\ value}{initial\ value} \times 100\%$
- $Water\ uptake\ rate\ (grams/hour) = \frac{change\ in\ mass}{time\ in\ minutes} \times 60$
- Linear graph has the equation $y = mx + c$
  - m is the gradient
  - c is the y-intercept

Plant stem cells 4.1.2.3

- In plant meristem tissue, stem cells can differentiate into any type of plant cell throughout the life of the plant.
- Plant stem cells are used to artificially produce clones of plants.
  - Quick and economic.
  - Rare species can be cloned to prevent extinction.
  - Crops with features such as disease resistance are cloned to make large numbers of identical plants for farmers.

Cell organisation, digestion, and enzymes

SNAPREVI

The digestive system 4.2.2.1

- $rate\ of\ reaction = \frac{amount\ of\ reactant\ used\ or\ product\ formed}{time\ taken}$
- The digestive system is an organ system.
- Digestion is the breakdown of large, insoluble food into small, soluble molecules, which are absorbed into the bloodstream.
- The products of digestion are used to build new carbohydrates, lipids and proteins. Some glucose is used in respiration.

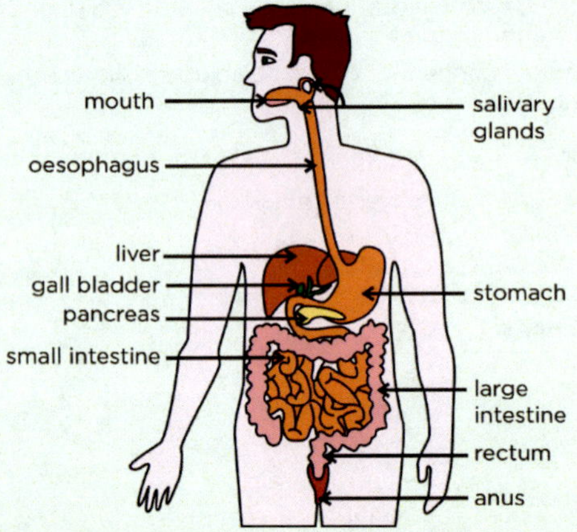

Structure	Function
Mouth	• Food ingested • Teeth chew food, breaking it into smaller pieces, increasing surface area for enzyme action
Salivary glands	Produce slightly alkaline saliva containing enzymes that break down starch
Oesophagus	Peristalsis (contraction and relaxation of circular and longitudinal muscles) moves food into the stomach
Stomach	• Churns the food with hydrochloric acid, killing microorganisms • Contains enzymes that break down protein
Small intestine	• Contains enzymes to break down food • Villi absorb the products of digestion • Glucose and amino acids are absorbed into the bloodstream (capillary) • Fatty acids and glycerol are absorbed into the lymph (lacteal)
Large intestine	• Absorbs remaining water, forming faeces
Rectum	• Stores faeces
Anus	• Egests faeces
Liver	• Produces bile
Gall bladder	• Stores bile
Pancreas	• Produces digestive enzymes

Cells, tissues, and organs 4.2.1

- Cells are the basic building blocks of all living organisms.
- Tissues are groups of cells with a similar structure and function.
- Organs are groups of tissues performing specific functions.
- An organ system is made up of organs.
- Organ systems work together to form organisms.

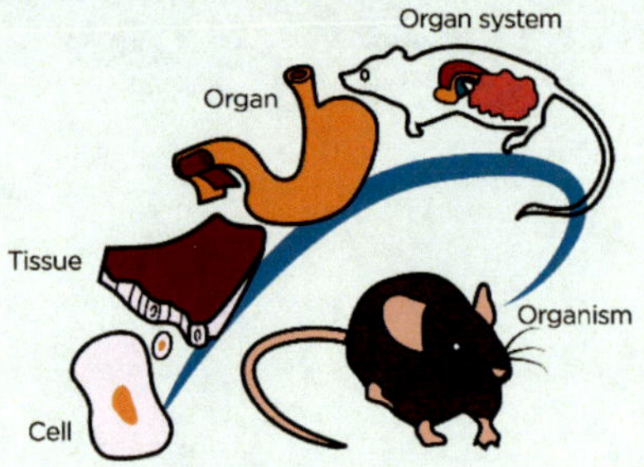

Digestive enzymes 4.2.2.1

- Saliva produced by salivary glands contains the carbohydrase enzymes amylase and maltase, which catalyses the breakdown of carbohydrates to simple sugars.
  - Amylase: $starch \rightarrow maltose$
  - Maltase: $maltose \rightarrow glucose$
- Proteases produced in the stomach begin the digestion of proteins into amino acids.
- Lipases break down lipids (fats and oils) into fatty acids and glycerol.
- The pancreas produces carbohydrase, protease and lipase enzymes and releases them into the small intestine.
- The liver produces bile, which is stored in the gall bladder.
- Bile neutralises the acid entering the small intestine from the stomach and emulsifies fats (breaks them up into small droplets, increasing the surface area for lipase action).

Lock and key theory 4.2.2.1

- Enzymes catalyse (speed up) specific reactions in organisms due to the shape of their active site.
- The substrate is the reactants of the reaction to be catalysed.
- The 'lock and key theory' proposes that the shape of the substrate is complementary to the active site so can bind to it, which allows the enzyme to break the bonds holding the substrate together.
- Enzyme-catalysed reactions contribute to metabolism.

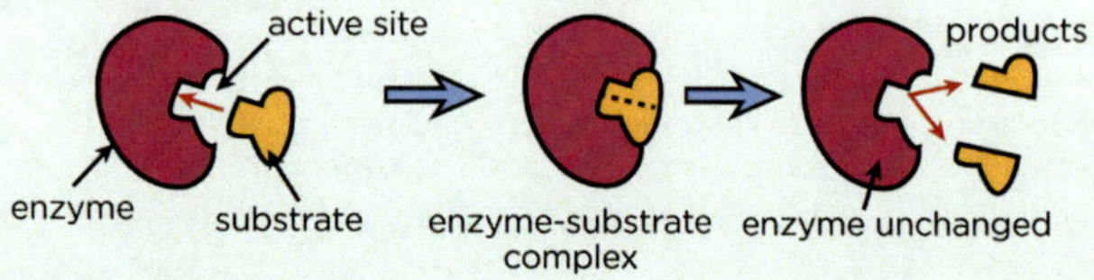

Denaturing enzymes 4.2.2

- Enzymes work at optimum conditions, and any movement away from these conditions lowers the enzyme activity and effectiveness.

Body part	Enzyme	Optimum pH	Optimum temperature
Mouth	Amylase, maltase	Alkaline	37 °C
Stomach	Protease	Acidic	37 °C
Small intestine	Lipase, protease, amylase, maltase	Alkaline	37 °C

- Enzymes are denatured by extremes of pH and temperature as the shape of the active site permanently changes so the substrate no longer fits.
- As temperature increases, enzymes and their substrate have more kinetic energy, so they will more frequently collide and enzyme activity increases.
- If temperature increases above the optimum temperature for enzyme, it will denature because the bonds holding it togethe will break.

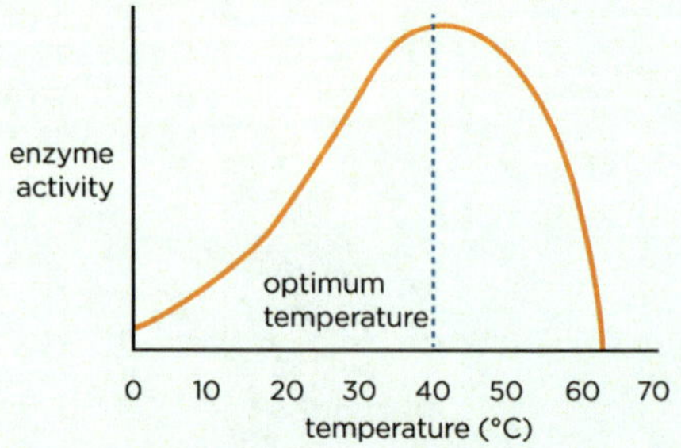

Active transport 4.1.3

- Active transport is the movement of substances from a more dilute solution to a more concentrated solution.
- As this movement is against a concentration gradient, it requires energy from respiration.
- Active transport facilitates:
  - The absorption of mineral ions from very dilute solutions in t soil into plant root hairs. Plants require ions for healthy grow
  - The absorption of sugar molecules from lower concentrations in the gut into the blood, which has a highe sugar concentration. Sugar molecules are needed for cell respiration.

he circulatory system

SNAPREVISE

Lung anatomy 4.2.2.2

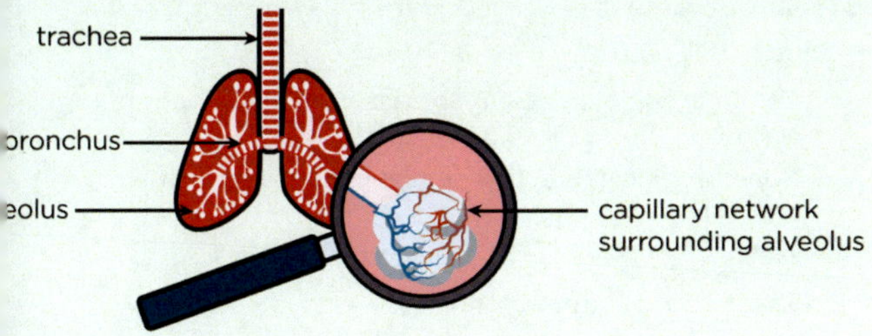

Carbon dioxide is removed from the blood in the lungs to prevent the pH of the blood becoming too acidic.

Lungs are adapted for gas exchange:

- Alveoli have a thin wall only one cell thick so there is a short distance for diffusion.
- Moist membrane accelerates the diffusion of gases.
- Shape of alveoli provides large surface area for diffusion.
- Extensive capillary network surrounding alveoli.
- Well-ventilated to maintain a large diffusion gradient.

Heart anatomy 4.2.2.2

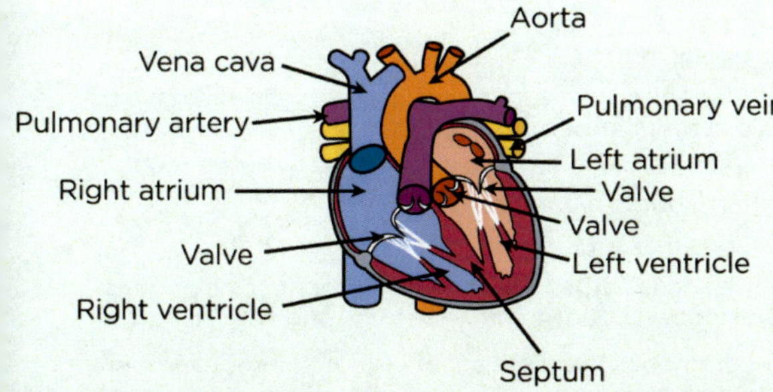

Valves prevent the backflow of blood.

The heart muscle cells are supplied by the coronary arteries, delivering oxygen for aerobic respiration to provide energy for the heart to contract.

The resting heart rate is controlled by a group of pacemaker cells ocated in the wall of the right atrium.

rregularities in the heart rate are corrected using artificial oacemakers, which are electrical devices.

The circulatory system 4.2.2.2

- The heart is an organ that pumps blood around the body in a double circulatory system (blood passes through the heart twice in one complete circuit of the body):
  - The right ventricle pumps deoxygenated blood to the lungs for gas exchange. Oxygen enters the blood and waste carbon dioxide leaves the blood.
  - The left ventricle pumps oxygenated blood around the rest of the body where body cells use the oxygen for aerobic respiration to provide energy.
  - Respiration also produces waste carbon dioxide, which is transported in the blood and exhaled via the lungs.

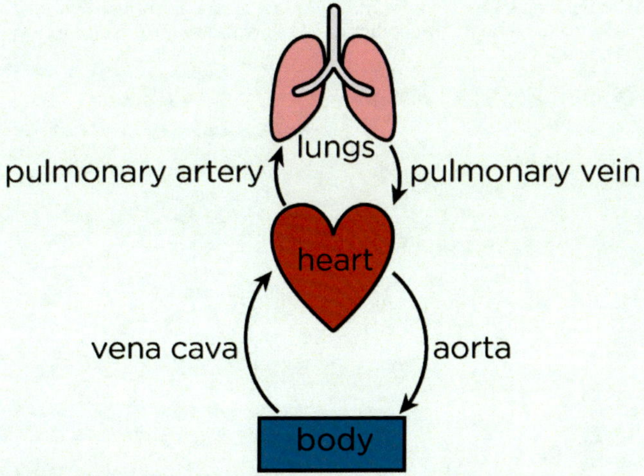

- Heart rate is the number of times the heart beats per minute.
- Stroke volume is the volume of blood ejected from the heart per heartbeat.
- Cardiac output is the volume of blood being pumped by the heart per minute.
- ***cardiac output = heart rate × stroke volume***

Blood vessels 4.2.2.2

Blood vessel	Function	Structure
Artery 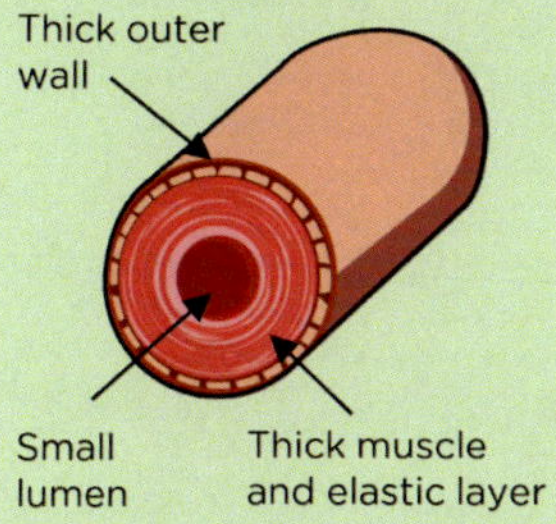	Transports oxygenated blood away from the heart at a high pressure so it can reach the rest of the body (apart from the pulmonary artery)	• Thick outer protective wall • Thick muscle and elastic layer that can stretch to withstand high-pressure blood flow • Small lumen to maintain high pressure • Smooth lining to minimise friction
Vein 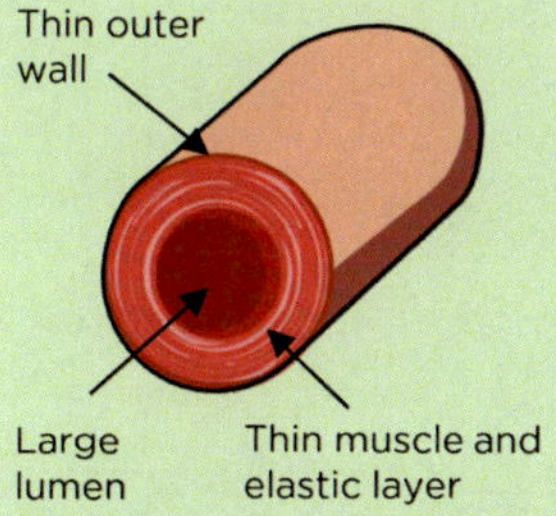	Transports deoxygenated blood back to the heart at a low pressure (apart from the pulmonary vein that carries oxygenated blood from the lungs)	• Thinner outer protective wall than artery as blood pressure is lower • Thin layer of muscle and elastic • Large lumen • Smooth lining to minimise friction • Valves to ensure blood flows one way
Capillary 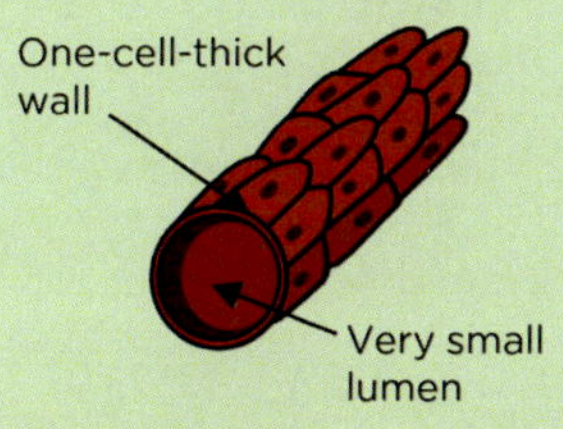	Surrounds respiring cells, transporting blood at a very low pressure so it moves slowly to allow time for gas exchange with neighbouring cells. Blood plasma passes through capillary walls into tissues where it is called tissue fluid.	• Very small lumen so blood is in contact with capillary wall to create a short distance of diffusion for gases • Capillary wall is one cell thick so there is a short distance of diffusion

Blood, heart problems, and human health

SNAPREVI

Blood 4.2.2.3

- Blood is a tissue.

Blood component	Function	Structure
Plasma	Other blood components are suspended in plasma, and it transports glucose, amino acids, carbon dioxide and urea	Straw-coloured aqueous liquid, mostly made from water, which dissolves nutrients
Red blood cells 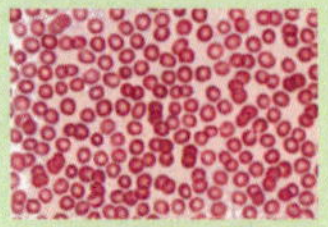	Transport oxygen around the body	• Contain haemoglobin, which binds to oxygen • Biconcave shape gives a high surface area to volume ratio • No nucleus to maximise space for more haemoglobin
White blood cells 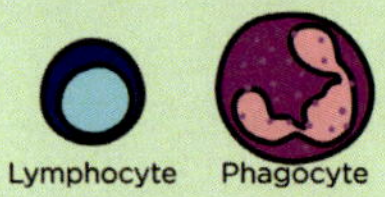 Lymphocyte Phagocyte	Part of immune system, which destroys pathogens: phagocytes engulf pathogens and digest them using enzymes, and lymphocytes produce antibodies to clump pathogens together	• Phagocytes have a lobed nucleus and a granulated cytoplasm (granules contain enzymes) • Lymphocytes are smaller, have a large nucleus and no granules
Platelets 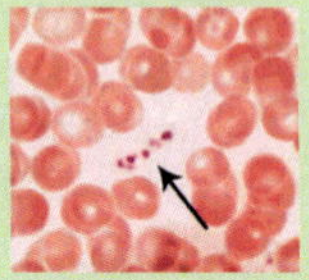	When the skin is wounded, they release clotting factors, which turn fibrinogen in the plasma into fibrin, forming a mesh that sticks platelets together to form a scab	Cell fragments containing chemicals called clotting factors

Coronary heart disease 4.2.2.4

- Coronary heart disease can lead to a heart attack:
  - Fatty material (plaque) builds up in the coronary arteries, narrowing them and reducing the flexibility of the artery lining, which reduces blood flow (atherosclerosis).
  - Less oxygen is delivered to the heart muscle.
  - Heart muscle cells die.
- Treatments for coronary heart disease:
  - Stents are used to keep the coronary arteries open.
  - Statins are used to reduce blood cholesterol levels to slow down the rate of fatty material deposit.

Other heart problems 4.2.2.4

- Faulty heart valves:
  - Prevent the valve from opening fully, and can leak.
  - Blood flows backwards, reducing the efficiency at which blood flows around the body, meaning cells do not receive as much glucose and oxygen for respiration.
  - Breathlessness, tiredness, dizziness and chest pain.
- Treatment of faulty heart valves:
  - Replace with biological valves from donors.
  - Replace with artificial mechanical valves.

Treating heart problems 4.2.2.4

- A donor heart, or heart and lungs, can be transplanted in the case of heart failure.
- Artificial hearts are sometimes used to keep patients alive whilst waiting for a heart transplant or to allow the heart to rest during recovery.

Treatment	Advantages	Disadvantages
Drugs	• Cheap • Can reduce cholesterol or reduce clotting	• Not suitable if you have liver disease • Side effects • Must be taken for life • Anti-blood clotting drugs increase the risk of bleeding
Mechanical	• Less dangerous than transplants • Fast recovery	• Biological valves may need to be replaced • Mechanical valves may cause blood clots
Transplant	• Lifesaving • Life can return to normal	• Slow recovery • Expensive operation • Risk of rejection by the immune system means the patient must take immunosuppressants for life • Few donor hearts available • Risky operation

Lowering risk of heart disease 4.2.2.6

- Lifestyle factors can increase the risk of cardiovascular disease:
  - Poor diet (high in fat and cholesterol)
  - Smoking
  - Alcohol
  - Lack of exercise
- Pre-existing conditions can increase the risk of cardiovascular disease:
  - Type 2 diabetes (of which obesity is a risk factor).
  - High blood pressure
  - High cholesterol

Physical and mental health 4.2.2

- Health is a state of physical and mental well-being.
- Causes of ill health:
  - Communicable disease (can pass from one organism to another)
  - Non-communicable disease (cannot pass from one organism another)
  - Diet
  - Stress and life situations
- Different types of disease may interact.
  - Defects in the immune system may mean an individual is mo likely to suffer from infectious diseases.
  - Immune reactions caused by a pathogen can trigger allergie such as skin rashes and asthma.
  - Viruses living in cells may trigger cancers.
  - Severe physical ill health can lead to mental illnesses, such as depression.

Lifestyle and risk 4.2.2

- Many diseases are caused by the interaction of multiple risk factors.
- Risk factors are linked to an increased rate of a disease, but a causal mechanism has not been proven for all of them. They include:
  - Lifestyle:
    - Alcohol is linked to degrading liver and brain function anc can harm unborn babies.
    - Smoking is linked to lung disease and lung cancer and ca harm unborn babies.
    - Obesity is a risk factor for Type 2 diabetes.
  - Substances in the body or environment (carcinogens, includi ionising radiation, are linked to causing cancer).
- Non-communicable diseases are more common in poorer areas inhabitants may be more exposed to negative risk factors, such lack of fresh food, water, and shelter, and may be more exposec to substances such as pollutants.
- Non-communicable diseases have a human and financial cost a local, national, and global levels:
  - Decrease quality of life and life expectancy.
  - Emotional and financial strains on friends and family if a pati is unable to work or to provide additional support.
  - Patient less productive at work, causing strain on the employ
  - Financial cost to health services to provide treatment and research.

ancer, plant tissues, and plant transport

Cancer 4.2.2.7

Cancer is the result of changes in cells that lead to uncontrolled growth and division.

Benign tumours are not cancers:

- Growth of abnormal cells, which are contained in one area, usually within a membrane
- Do not invade other parts of the body

Malignant tumours are cancers:

- Invade neighbouring tissues
- Spread to different parts of the body in the blood where they form secondary tumours (by metastasis)
- Signs of cancer include tumorous lumps, a long-term cough and unexplained bleeding or weight loss

Different cancers have different risk factors:

- Smoking and alcohol
- Obesity
- Age
- Infections, such as hepatitis and HPV
- Ionising radiation (e.g. UV from the sun)
- Environmental pollutants from industry
- Genetic disorders inherited from parents

Cancer can be screened (e.g. blood tests and X-ray images).

Cancer may be treated with chemotherapy and radiotherapy; however, this can kill healthy cells too, with side effects including sickness and hair loss.

Xylem and phloem 4.2.3.2

Xylem and phloem found together in the vascular bundle.

Xylem tissue transports water and mineral ions up from the roots to the leaves via the stem.

- Hollow tubes without end walls.
- Tube walls strengthened by lignin.

Phloem tissue transports dissolved sucrose from the leaves (made from glucose from photosynthesis) to the rest of the plant for use or storage. This is called translocation.

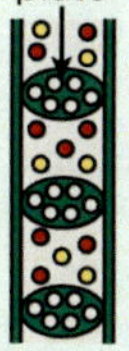

- Tubes of living elongated cells.
- Cell sap can move from one cell to the next through pores in the end walls.

Plant tissues 4.2.3.1

- The roots, stem and leaves form a plant organ system for transport of substances around the plant.
- The leaf is a plant organ made up of numerous plant tissues.

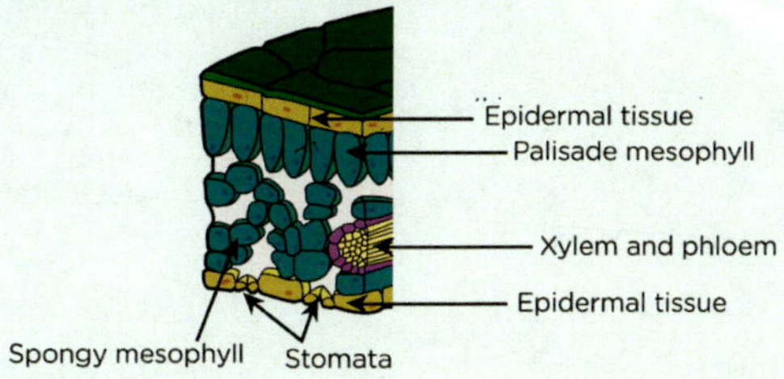

Tissue	Function	Structure
Epidermal tissues	• Protects against water loss • Regulates gas exchange in leaves • Regulates water and mineral uptake in roots	• Outermost layer one cell thick and transparent to allow light to easily pass through • Contains stomata and guard cells on bottom of leaf
Palisade mesophyll	Major site of photosynthesis	• Found towards upper surface of leaf so lots of light reaches it • Tightly-packed cells containing lots of chloroplast to maximise photosynthesis
Spongy mesophyll	Gas exchange	• Found towards bottom of leaves close to where gas enters through stomata • Space between cells to allow gases to diffuse • Cells have a large surface area in contact with air spaces to maximise gas exchange
Meristem tissue	Stem cells are produced for plant growth	• Found at the growing tips of shoots and roots

Root hair cells 4.2.3.2

- Root hair cells are adapted for the efficient uptake of water by osmosis and mineral ions by active transport:
  - Thin – short distance for osmosis and active transport.
  - Long – penetrate between soil particles to come into contact with water and mineral ions.
  - Large surface area – maximise osmosis and active transport.
  - Lots of mitochondria for active transport.

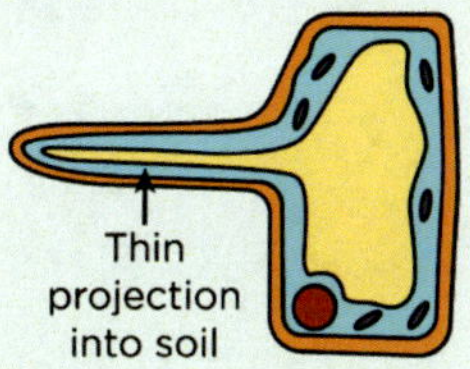

Transpiration and translocation 4.2.3.2

- The movement of water through a plant occurs through transpiration, where water is pulled through the plant as it is continuously released from the leaves through stomata.
  - Water enters the root hair cells by osmosis and travels through them to the xylem.
  - Water travels up the xylem in the stem into the spongy mesophyll of the leaf by osmosis.
  - Water evaporates out of spongy mesophyll cells, forming water vapour in the air spaces of the spongy mesophyll.
  - Water vapour diffuses out of the leaf through stomata.
- Stomata control gas exchange and water loss by opening and closing, which is controlled by guard cells.
  - When guard cells are turgid, the stomata are open, allowing water vapour to leave the leaf and carbon dioxide to enter for photosynthesis.
  - When dehydrated, guard cells are flaccid and the stomata are closed, preventing further water loss.
- $\textit{Transpiration rate} = \dfrac{\textit{decrease in mass or volume of water absorbed}}{\textit{time}}$

- Transpiration rate is affected by various factors:

Factor	Effect on transpiration rate
Temperature	Transpiration rate increases as temperature increases because molecules have greater kinetic energy, speeding up the rate of evaporation and diffusion.
Humidity	Transpiration rate decreases as humidity increases as the atmosphere has a higher concentration of water vapour, decreasing the diffusion of water vapour out of the leaf.
Air movement	Transpiration rate increases as wind increases as it carries water vapour from the leaf.
Light intensity	Transpiration rate increases as light intensity increases as the stomata open wider to allow carbon dioxide in for photosynthesis, allowing water vapour to escape.

Pathogens 4.3.1.1

- Pathogens are microorganisms (viruses, bacteria, protists, and fungi) that cause infectious disease.
- There are various ways a disease can be spread in animals and plants:
  - Direct contact – spread by physical contact
  - Transfer of infected fluids, e.g. blood, saliva, semen
  - Contaminated water – travels in unsterilised water
  - Airborne – propelled through the air in tiny droplets of water through sneezing and coughing
  - Food – pathogens in uncooked or spoiled food
  - Via another animal – the animal is called a vector
- The spread of disease can be reduced or prevented by:
  - Sterilising water with chemicals or UV light
  - Cooking food thoroughly and preparing it in hygienic conditions
  - Disinfecting surfaces
  - Treating infections, e.g. with antibiotics
  - Vaccination
  - Barrier method of contraception to prevent the spread of sexually transmitted diseases, e.g. condom
- Bacteria and viruses can reproduce rapidly inside the body.
  - Bacteria can produce toxins that damage tissues and cause disease symptoms.
  - Viruses live and reproduce inside cells, causing cell damage.

Non-specific immunity 4.3.1.6

- Humans have non-specific defence systems to prevent pathogens from entering the body:
  - Skin – forms a physical barrier to prevent pathogens from entering the body, secretes antimicrobial compounds to kill pathogens, and sheds dead surface skin, which removes pathogens.
  - Tears and saliva – contain antibacterial lysozymes, which break down bacterial cell walls.
  - Nose – contains hairs acting as a filter, preventing large particles from passing through and producing sticky mucus that traps pathogens and is removed when you blow your nose.
  - Trachea and bronchi – lined with ciliated cells and goblet cells to prevent pathogens from entering the lungs. Goblet cells produce mucus to trap pathogens and cilia (tiny hair-like projections) rhythmically beat the mucus up the airway to the back of the throat where it is swallowed.
  - Stomach – contains hydrochloric acid, which destroys swallowed pathogens.

Viral diseases 4.3.1.2

Disease	Symptoms	Transmission	Details
Measles	Fever and red skin rash	Airborne: inhalation of droplets from sneezes and coughs	• Can be fatal if complications arise • Most young children are vaccinated against measles
HIV	Initially causes flu-like symptoms	Transfer of infected fluids: transfer of bodily fluids during sex or exchange of blood, e.g. in blood transfusion or when drug users share needles	• Unless controlled with antiretroviral drugs, the virus attacks immune cells • Damage to the immune system causes AIDS as it can no longer deal with other infections or cancers
Tobacco mosaic virus (TMV)	Distinctive 'mosaic' pattern of discolouration on leaves	Direct contact: rubbing of leaf against an infected leaf	• Affecting many species of plants including tomatoes • Affects growth of plant due to lack of photosynthesis

Bacterial diseases 4.3.1

Disease	Symptoms	Transmission	Details
Salmonella	Fever, abdominal cramps, vomiting and diarrhoea	Ingesting spoiled food or food prepared in unhygienic conditions	• Food poisoning • In the UK, poultr are vaccinated against salmonel to control the spread
Gonorrhoea	Thick yellow or green discharge from the vagina or penis and pain when urinating	Sexual contact (STD)	• Was easily treate with penicillin un many resistant strains appeared • Treated with antibiotics and prevented by usi barrier method c contraception

Fungal diseases 4.3.1

Disease	Symptoms	Transmission	Details
Rose black spot	Purple or black spots develop on leaves, which often turn yellow and fall early	Water or wind	• Affects the grow of the plant as photosynthesis i reduced • Treated using fungicides and removing and destroying the infected plant tissue

Protist diseases 4.3.

Disease	Symptoms	Transmission	Details
Malaria	Recurrent episodes of fever, which can be fatal	Vector – protist carried by mosquito	• Can be fatal • Spread controlle by preventing mosquitos from breeding and us mosquito nets tc avoid being bitte

SNAPREVISE

The immune system 4.3.1.6

f pathogens make it past the non-specific defence system and enter the body, the immune system will coordinate a response to destroy them.

White blood cells defend against pathogens by:

- Phagocytosis:

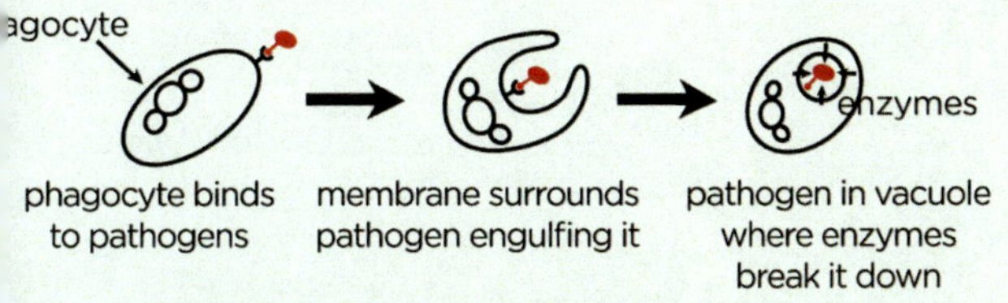

- Antibody production – lymphocytes detect foreign antigens (proteins on surface of cells) on pathogens and respond by producing antibodies.
- Antibodies are specific to each antigen and bind to the antigens of multiple pathogens to clump them together for phagocytosis.
- If infected by the same pathogen again, memory lymphocytes recognise the antigens and produce a larger number of specific antibodies faster.

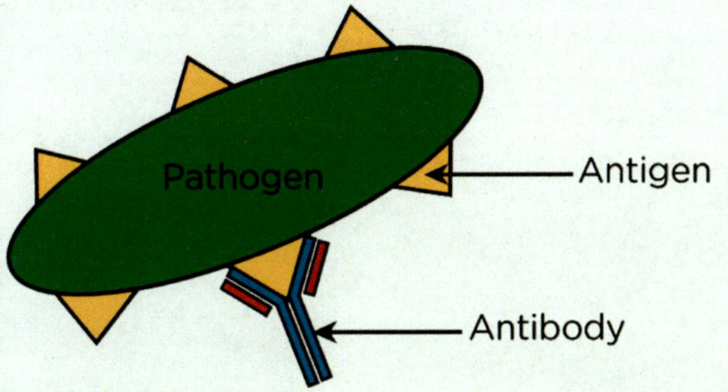

Antitoxin production – Lymphocytes form a special antibody called antitoxins, which bind to and neutralise harmful toxins produced by the pathogen.

Vaccination 4.3.1.7

- Vaccination introduces a small amount of dead or inactive forms of a pathogen into the body:
  - This stimulates the production of antibodies.
  - If the pathogen enters the body again, memory lymphocytes will recognise the antigens of the pathogen and produce a larger number of specific antibodies faster.
  - The pathogen is destroyed before the person becomes ill.
- Herd immunity is where the spread of pathogens can be reduced by immunising a large proportion of the population, meaning the disease is unlikely to spread.

Antibiotics 4.3.1.8

- Antibiotics are medicines used to treat bacterial diseases.
  - Penicillin is an antibiotic produced by a fungus, which kills bacteria by weakening their cell walls so they burst.
  - Some alter bacterial enzymes.
  - Some stop bacteria from reproducing.
- Specific antibiotics are used to kill specific bacteria, and they cannot kill viruses.
- Antibiotics have greatly reduced deaths from bacterial diseases.

Causes of antibiotic resistance 4.3.1.8

- Some strains of bacteria have evolved resistance to antibiotics.
- Drug companies are constantly researching new antibiotics or alternatives for resistant strains.
- Over-prescription of antibiotics has contributed to the emergence of these resistant strains.

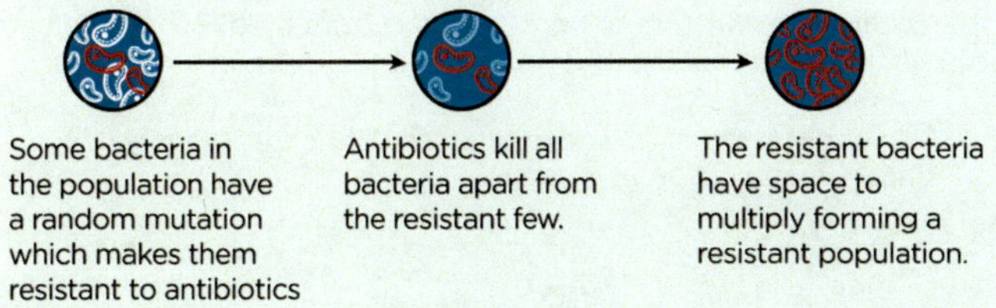

Painkillers 4.3.1.8

- Painkillers and other medicines treat the symptoms of disease but do not kill pathogens.
- It is difficult to develop drugs that destroy viruses without also damaging the body's tissues, as viruses are active within human body cells.

Historical drugs 4.3.1.9

- Drugs were traditionally extracted from plants and microorganisms:
  - The painkiller aspirin comes from the willow tree.
  - The heart drug digitalis comes from foxgloves.
  - Penicillin was discovered accidentally by Alexander Fleming from the Penicillium mould, which contaminated his petri dish of bacteria.

Modern drug development 4.3.1.9

- Most modern drugs are artificially synthesised by chemists in the pharmaceutical industry, e.g. paracetamol.

Stage in drug development	Description
Identifying potential drug	May be a chemical extracted from another organism, e.g. plant.
Computer modelling	Modelling the drug's structure and potential interactions with substances in the body.
Preclinical testing	• Done in a laboratory using live cells, tissues and live animals. • Checks the drugs are safe and effective, with tests for toxicity and efficiency.
Clinical trials	• First phase uses healthy volunteers to test toxicity. • Very low doses of the drug are given at the start of the trial. • If the drug is safe, it will be given to a small number of sick patients in phase two to test efficacy. • Phase three trials use larger numbers of patients and finalise safe, optimum doses. • In double-blind trials, some patients are given a placebo to test whether the drug is causing the improvement in patients or if it is just the placebo effect.
Manufacturing	The drug is produced on a mass scale and made available to the public.

Monoclonal antibodies and plant disease

Plant disease identification 4.3.3.1

- Symptoms of plant disease include:
  - Stunted growth
  - Spots on leaves
  - Rot (areas of decay)
  - Abnormal growths
  - Malformed stem or leaves
  - Discolouration
  - The presence of pests
- Plant disease can be identified by:
  - Research using a gardening manual or website
  - Taking the infected plant to a laboratory to identify the pathogen
  - Using monoclonal antibody testing kits

Plant disease examples 4.3.3.1

- Plants can be infected by viral, bacterial and fungal pathogens and insects.
- Aphids are insects that tap into the phloem of plant stems with very fine mouthparts (stylet) to ingest the sap.
  - This deprives the plant of its nutrient source.
  - Plant growth rate decreases and the plant wilts.
  - Can be prevented by increasing the number of ladybirds in your garden as they eat aphids, rather than spraying insecticides.

Disease	Type	Symptoms	Details
Tobacco mosaic virus	Viral disease transmitted by rubbing of leaf against the infected leaf.	Distinctive 'mosaic' pattern of discolouration on leaves	• Affecting many species of plants, including tomatoes • Affects growth of plant due to lack of photosynthesis
Black spot	Fungal disease transmitted by water or wind	Purple or black spots develop on leaves, which often turn yellow and fall	• Affects the growth of the plant as photosynthesis is reduced • Treated using fungicides and removing the affected leaves

Plant nutrient deficiencies 4.3.3.1

- Mineral ions are absorbed from the soil by the roots.
- Nitrate ions are needed for protein synthesis and therefore growth. Hence, nitrate deficiency causes stunted growth.
- Magnesium ions are needed to make chlorophyll for photosynthesis. Therefore, magnesium deficiency causes chlorosis (yellow leaves).

Plant defences 4.3.3.2

- Plants have mechanical adaptations and physical and chemical defence responses to aid survival.
- Physical defence responses:
  - Cellulose cell walls act as a barrier to pathogens.
  - Tough waxy cuticle on leaves to control water loss also acts as a barrier to pathogens.
  - Layers of undigestible dead cells around stems (bark on trees) prevent plant being eaten by herbivores, and dead cells eventually fall off, taking pathogens with them.
- Chemical plant defence responses:
  - Antibacterial chemicals, such as in tea tree leaves.
  - Poisons to prevent being eaten by herbivores, such as in deadly nightshade.
- Mechanical adaptations:
  - Thorns and spines to prevent being eaten by herbivores.
  - Leaves that droop or curl when touched, knocking insects off.
  - Mimicry to trick animals, e.g. some species have spotted leaves that look like butterfly eggs, which prevents butterflies from egg-laying so as to avoid competition.

Producing monoclonal antibodies 4.3.2.1

- Monoclonal antibodies are a large population of identical antibodies.
- The antibodies are specific to one protein antigen and so target a specific chemical or cell in the body. Once the antibody is bound, the target can easily be detected or targeted for treatment.
- Monoclonal antibodies are produced from a single clone of cells.
  - An antigen is injected into a mouse. This stimulates the mouse lymphocytes to make an antibody specific to this antigen.
  - The lymphocytes are collected from spleen cells.
  - The lymphocytes are combined with myeloma tumour cells to make hybridoma cells.
  - The hybridoma cells are grown in a culture medium indefinitely, where they replicate and produce large amounts of the antibody.
  - The antibody is collected and purified by centrifugation, filtration and chromatography.

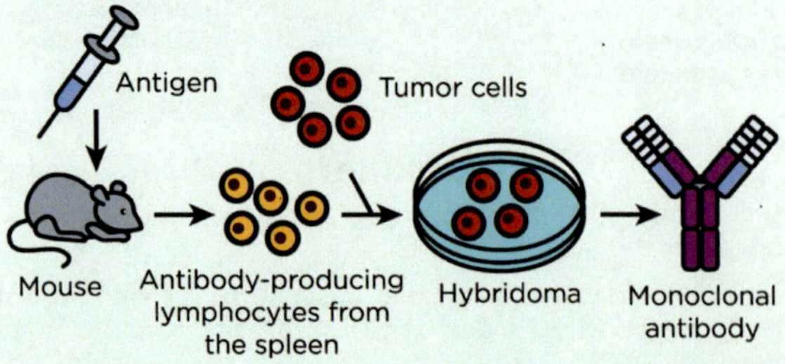

Using monoclonal antibodies 4.3.2

- Monoclonal antibodies have many uses

Use	Description
Pregnancy tests	• HCG is a hormone found in the urine of pregnant peopl • The person suspecting pregnancy urinates on a small stick of paper containing a strip of monoclonal antibodies specific to HCG. • If the person is pregnant, HCG in the urine binds to the antibodies. The test the turns a different colour.
To detect pathogens or measure the levels of hormones and chemicals in blood, in a laboratory	• Antibodies are bound to a fluorescent dye. • When antibodies bind to the antigen and are viewed under UV light, they glow.
In research to locate or identify a specific molecule in cells or tissues	• Antibodies are tagged with a fluorescent dye and are specific to the molecule to be identified/located.
To treat disease	• In cancer treatment, the monoclonal antibody is bound to a radioactive substance, toxic drug or chemical, which stops cancerous cells growing an dividing. • The antibody binds specifically to the cancer cells, delivering these substances without harmin other body cells.

- However, monoclonal antibodies create more side effects than expected, so are not as widely used as people may have hopec

hotosynthesis, respiration, and metabolism

SNAPREVISE

Response to exercise 4.4.2.2

During exercise, the human body reacts to the increased demand for energy:

- Heart rate, breathing rate and breath volume increase to supply the muscles with more oxygenated blood so they can carry out maximum aerobic respiration to release energy for movement.
- If insufficient oxygen is supplied, anaerobic respiration takes place in muscles to provide energy, causing a build-up of lactic acid, which causes cramps and muscle fatigue, so they stop contracting efficiently.
- Blood flowing through the muscles transports the lactic acid to the liver where it is converted back into glucose.
- Oxygen debt is the amount of extra oxygen required after exercise to react with lactic acid to remove it from cells.

Metabolism 4.4.2.3

Metabolism is the sum of all the reactions in a cell or the body.

- Conversion of glucose to starch, glycogen, and cellulose.
- The formation of lipid molecules from a molecule of glycerol and three molecules of fatty acids.
- The use of glucose and nitrate ions to form the amino acids needed to synthesise proteins.
- Respiration.
- Digestion (breakdown of carbohydrates, proteins, and lipids).
- Breakdown of excess proteins to form urea for excretion.

The energy released by cellular respiration is used by the organism for the continual enzyme-controlled processes of metabolism that synthesise new molecules.

Photosynthesis 4.4.1.1

Photosynthesis is an endothermic reaction where light energy from the environment is transferred into the chloroplasts.

Chlorophyll is the green pigment in chloroplasts, which absorb light energy for photosynthesis.

Photosynthesis is carried out by the plant to produce glucose, which has many uses including plant respiration.

Word equation:

$$carbon\ dioxide + water \xrightarrow{light} glucose + oxygen$$

Symbol equation: $CO_2 + H_2O \xrightarrow{light} C_6H_{12}O_6 + 6O_2$

Rate of photosynthesis 4.4.1.2

- $rate\ of\ photosynthesis = \frac{volume\ of\ oxygen\ produced\ or\ carbon\ dioxide\ absorbed}{time}$
- There are various factors that can affect the rate of photosynthesis.

Factor	Effect on photosynthesis rate
Temperature	• Increases as temperature increases, as molecules have more kinetic energy, so they collide more often and react faster. • Decreases at temperatures that are too high as the enzymes involved in photosynthesis denature.
Light intensity	• Increases as light intensity increases, as light energy is needed for the reaction. • If the distance between the plant and light is doubled, the rate is quartered (inverse square law): $light\ intensity \propto \frac{1}{distance^2}$
Carbon dioxide concentration	Increases as concentration increases, as carbon dioxide is needed for reaction.
Amount of chlorophyll	Increases as chlorophyll amount increases, as chlorophyll absorbs light energy needed for reaction.

- These factors interact and the one that limits the reaction rate of photosynthesis is known as the limiting factor, meaning the rate cannot increase further without changing that condition.

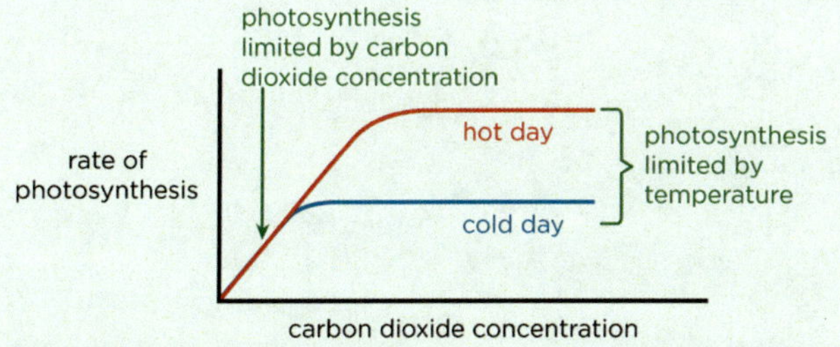

- Limiting factors are important in the economics of enhancing the conditions in greenhouses to gain the maximum rate of photosynthesis while still maintaining a profit.
  - For example, if the rate of photosynthesis is only limited by the current light intensity, increasing the temperature in the greenhouse will not have much of an effect.

Uses of glucose 4.4.1.3

- The glucose produced in photosynthesis may be:
  - Used for respiration to provide energy for the plant.
  - Converted into insoluble starch for storage for later use.
  - Used to produce fat or oil for storage.
  - Used to produce cellulose, which strengthens the cell wall.
  - Used to produce amino acids for protein synthesis and growth, which also requires nitrate ions from the soil.

Aerobic respiration 4.4.2.1

- Cellular respiration is an exothermic reaction as it releases energy. It is continuously occurring in living cells to provide all the energy needed for living processes.
- Aerobic respiration uses oxygen.
- Energy is released from glucose by completely oxidising it.
- Word equation: $glucose + oxygen \rightarrow carbon\ dioxide + water$
- Symbol equation: $C_6H_{12}O_6 + 6O_2 \rightarrow 6CO_2 + 6H_2O$

Anaerobic respiration 4.4.2.1

- Anaerobic respiration takes place without oxygen.
- As it is the incomplete oxidation of glucose, much less energy is released than in aerobic respiration.
- Anaerobic respiration takes place in muscles in humans.
  - Word equation: $glucose \rightarrow lactic\ acid$
  - The incomplete oxidation of glucose produces lactic acid.
- Anaerobic respiration takes place in plant and yeast cells.
  - Word equation: $glucose \rightarrow ethanol + carbon\ dioxide$
  - Anaerobic respiration in yeast cells is called fermentation and is used in the manufacture of bread and alcoholic drinks.

Uses of energy 4.4.2.1

- Organisms need energy for:
  - Chemical reactions to build larger molecules.
  - Movement.
  - Keeping warm.

Homeostasis 4.5.1

- Homeostasis is the regulation of the internal conditions of a cell or organism to maintain optimum conditions for enzyme activity and all cellular functions in response to internal and external changes.
- In humans, homeostasis includes control of:
  - Blood glucose concentration (too low and you would not release enough energy in respiration, too high and you go into a coma).
  - Body temperature (too low and your enzymes will have a low kinetic energy and reactions would take place too slowly, too high and enzymes would denature and be unable to catalyse reactions).
  - Water levels (too low and your cells will shrink, too high and your cells will burst).
- Automatic control systems, involving nervous or chemical responses, are used to maintain homeostasis.
  - Responses involving the nervous system happen very quickly using electrical impulses.
  - Responses involving the hormonal system are slower as the hormones travel in the blood.
- Control systems include:
  - Receptor cells, which detect the stimulus (the change in the environment).
  - Coordination centres, which receive and process information from receptors (such as the brain, spinal cord, and pancreas),
  - Effectors, which bring about responses that restore optimum levels (muscles or glands).

The nervous system 4.5.2.1

- The nervous system enables humans to react to their surroundings and to coordinate their behaviour.

Stimulus → Receptor —(neurones)→ Coordinator (CNS) —(neurones)→ Effector (muscles/glands) → Response

- The stimulus is the change that the body must respond to.
- The receptor is the cell or part of a cell that detects the change and generates an electrical impulse.
- The information passes along neurone cells as electrical impulses to the central nervous system (CNS).
- The CNS is made up of the brain and spinal cord and coordinates the response involving effectors.
- The effector response may involve causing muscles to contract or glands to secrete hormones.

Nerves and neurones 4.5.2.1

- A bundle of neurones running parallel to each other forms a nerve.
- A fatty layer called the myelin sheath acts as insulation around sensory and motor neurones, speeding up the speed of electrical transmission.

Sensory neurones carry electrical impulses from the receptor to the CNS.

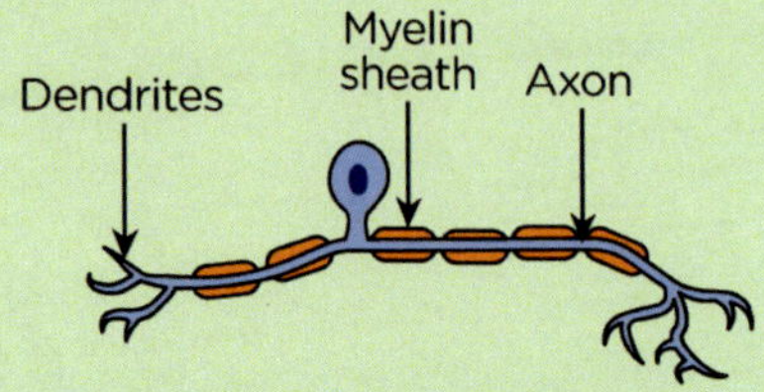

Relay neurones carry electrical impulses through the CNS.

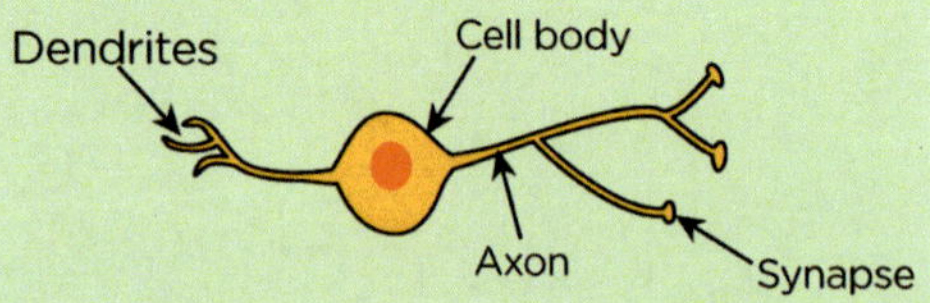

Motor neurones carry electrical impulses from the CNS to an effector (muscle or gland).

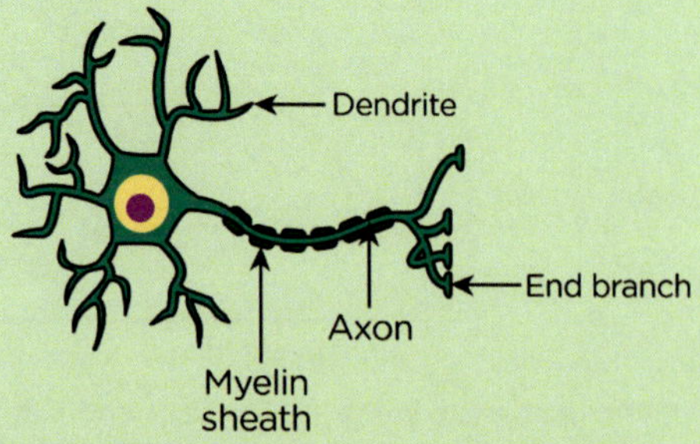

Synapses 4.5.

- Electrical impulses move from one neurone to the next at junctions called synapses.
  - An electrical impulse reaches the end of an axon's branch.
  - The end branches convert the electrical impulse into a chemical signal called neurotransmitters, which diffuse acros the synapse.
  - The neurotransmitters bind to the receptors on the dendrites the neighbouring neurone, triggering the start of an electrica impulse in this neurone.
  - Once bound to receptors, the neurotransmitter is broken dov by enzymes to prevent the second neurone from continually sending new electrical impulses.

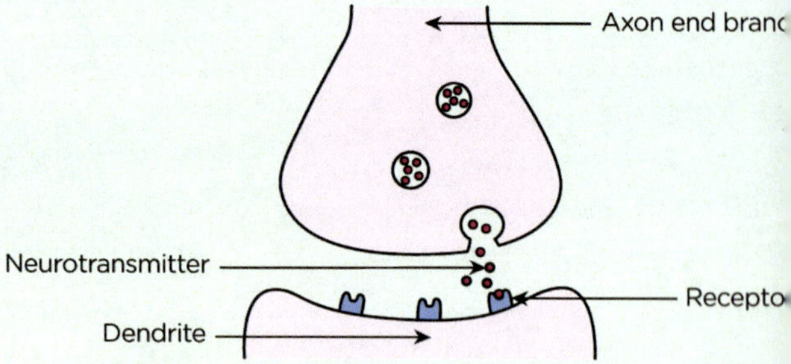

Reflex arcs 4.5.

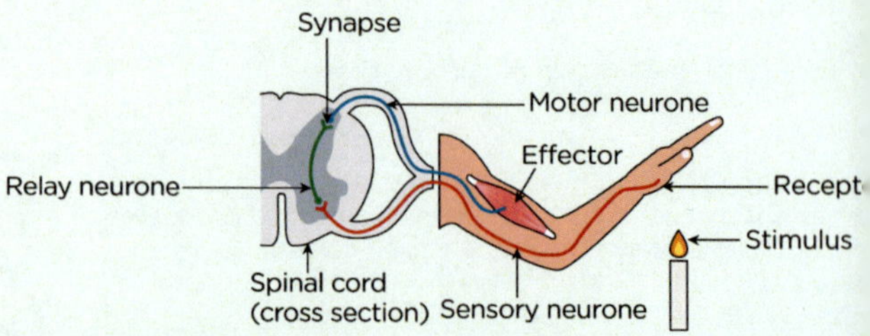

- Reflex actions take place to stop you damaging your body by mistake, in order to prevent or minimise damage, e.g. moving your hand away from a flame when pain and heat receptors ser burning.
- Reflex actions are automatic and rapid as they go through relay neurones in the spinal cord and do not involve the conscious pa of the brain, meaning time is not taken sending the information there.
- Reflex responses also occur to coordinate internal processes without conscious thought, e.g. regulate heart rate and control pupil size.
- Reaction time is the time it takes to respond to a stimulus.

The brain 4.5.2.2

The brain controls complex behaviour. It is made of billions of nterconnected neurones and has different regions that carry out different functions.

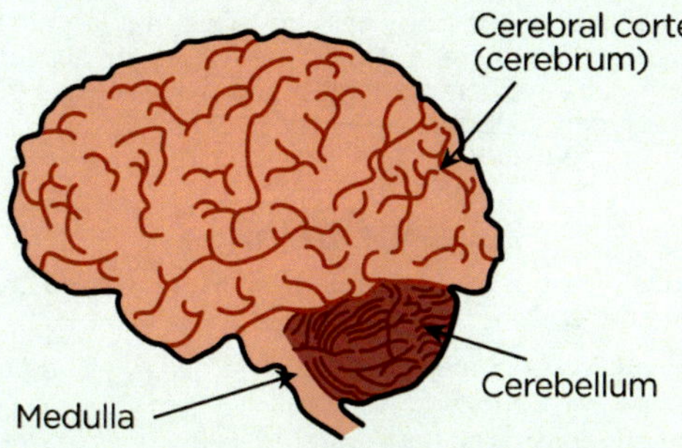

Brain region	Function
Cerebral cortex	Divided into left and right hemispheres, responsible for consciousness, memories, intelligence, and the ability to use language.
Cerebellum	Controls and coordinates the movements of muscles.
Medulla	Controls unconscious (automatic or involuntary) activities, e.g. heart rate and breathing.

Studying the brain 4.5.2.2

The complexity and delicacy of the brain make investigating and reating brain disorders difficult.

- Brain surgery is risky and may cause side effects or further damage.
- Brain-damaged patients may not be able to consent.

Neuroscientists have mapped the regions of the brain to particular functions by studying patients with brain damage, using non-invasive techniques, such as electrically stimulating different parts of the brain, and using MRI scanning techniques.

The eye 4.5.2.3

- The eye is a sense organ that contains receptors sensitive to light intensity and colour.

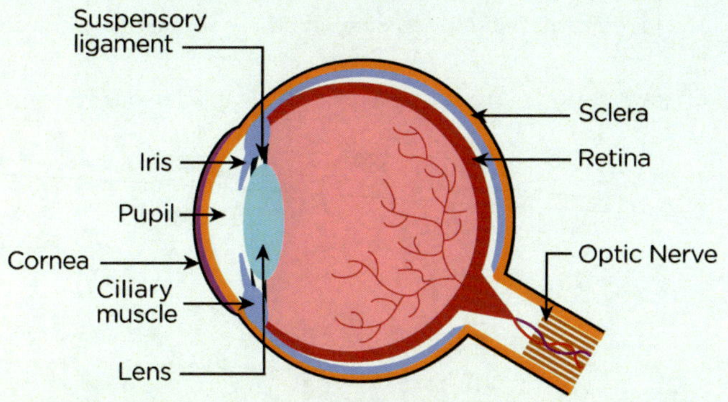

Structure	Function
Retina	Contains light-sensitive receptor cells: rods and cones that convert light into an electrical impulse. Cones allow you to see in colour when light intensity is high (daytime), while rods work in lower light intensities (night-time) but only enable black and white vision.
Optic nerve	Carries electrical impulses from the eye to the brain to generate an 'image'.
Sclera	Outer layer that protects the eye. White in humans.
Cornea	Transparent layer that refracts light through the pupil.
Iris	Muscles surrounding the pupil that control the size of the pupil. Muscles contract and relax to control how much light enters the eye.
Lens	Changes shape to focus light on the retina.
Ciliary muscles	Contract and relax to change the shape of the lens.
Suspensory ligaments	Loosen and pull tight to change the shape of the lens.

Accommodation 4.5.2.3

- Accommodation is the automatic process of changing the shape of the lens to focus on near or distant objects.
- To focus on a near object:
  - The ciliary muscles contract.
  - The suspensory ligaments loosen.
  - The lens becomes shorter and thicker, refracting light rays strongly.
- To focus on a distant object:
  - The ciliary muscles relax.
  - The suspensory ligaments are pulled tight.
  - The lens is pulled thinner and longer and only slightly refracts light rays.

Adaptation to dim light 4.5.2.3

- When light intensity is low (e.g. at night) the pupil becomes larger (dilates) in a reflex response to maximise the amount of light entering the eye.
  - The muscles in the iris increase the size of the pupil (dilated pupils).
  - Radial muscles contract.
  - Circular muscles relax.
- The opposite takes place in bright light, to prevent too much light from entering and damaging the eye.

Myopia and hyperopia 4.5.2.3

- Sometimes rays of light do not focus on the retina.
  - Myopia is short-sightedness.
  - Hyperopia is long-sightedness.
- These defects are treated with spectacle lenses (glasses), which refract the light rays so that they focus on the retina.
- New technologies include hard and soft contact lenses, laser surgery to change the shape of the cornea and a replacement lens in the eye.

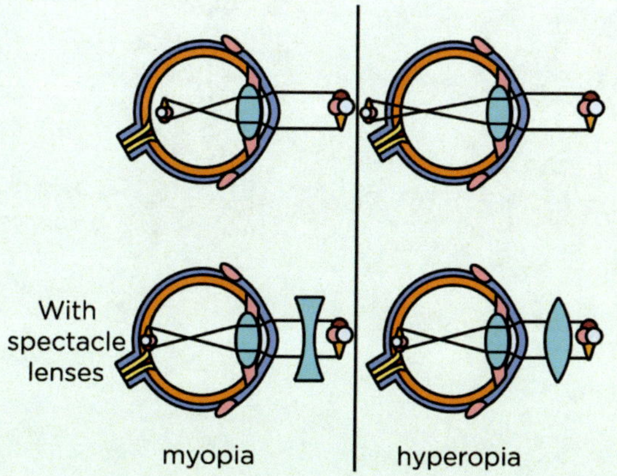

Thermoregulation 4.5.2.4

- Body temperature is monitored and controlled by the thermoregulatory centre in the brain.
- The thermoregulatory centre contains receptors sensitive to the temperature of the blood.
- The skin contains temperature receptors and sends nervous impulses to the thermoregulatory centre.
- If the body temperature is too high:
  - Arterioles near the skin's surface dilate (vasodilation), increasing blood flow so more heat is lost from the body via convection, conduction, and radiation.
  - Sweat is produced from sweat glands, so energy is taken from the body as it evaporates.
- If the body temperature is too low:
  - Arterioles near the surface of the skin constrict (vasoconstriction), minimising blood flow and heat loss.
  - Sweating stops.
  - Skeletal muscles involuntarily contract and relax quickly (shiver) to generate heat.

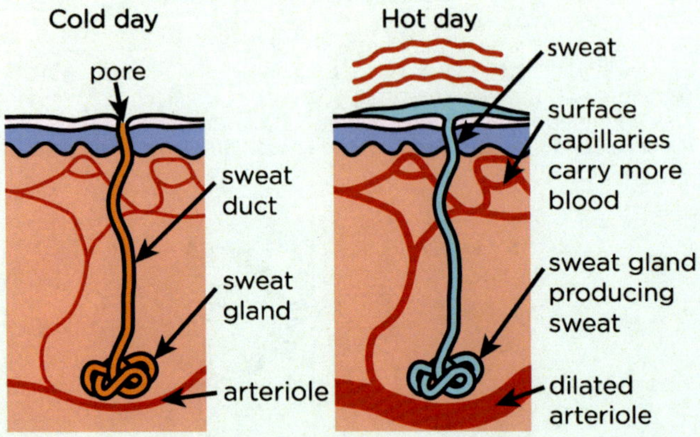

The endocrine system 4.5.3.1

- The endocrine system is composed of glands, which secrete chemicals called hormones directly into the bloodstream.
- The blood carries hormones to target organs where they produce an effect.
- Effects are slower but longer lasting than in the nervous system.

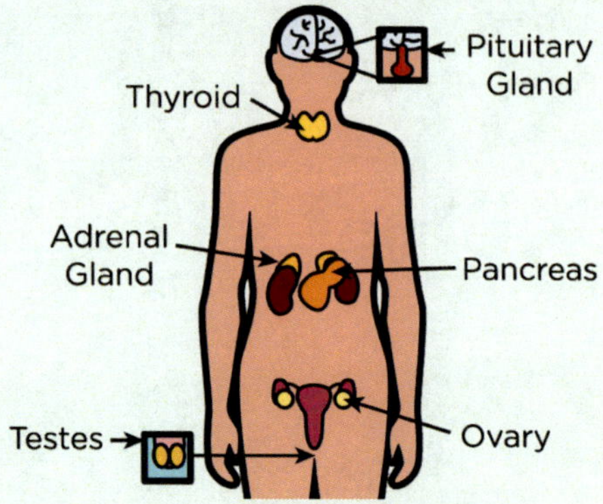

The pituitary gland 4.5.3.1

- The pituitary gland is a 'master gland' found in the brain.
- It secretes several hormones into the blood in response to body conditions.
- The hormones it secretes act on other glands to stimulate other hormones to be released to bring about effects.

Control of blood glucose 4.5.3.2

- Blood glucose concentration is monitored and controlled by the pancreas.
  - If the blood glucose concentration is too high, the pancreas produces the hormone insulin to return it to normal levels.
  - Insulin causes glucose to move from the blood into the cells, and excess glucose is converted to glycogen for storage in liver and muscle cells.
  - If the blood glucose concentration is too low, the pancreas produces the hormone glucagon, which causes glycogen to be converted into glucose to be released into the blood.
- Control of blood glucose concentration by insulin and glucagon occurs via a negative feedback cycle as the body detects a change from the optimum and makes an adjustment to return it back to normal.

Diabetes 4.5.3

- Type 1 diabetes is a disorder in which the pancreas fails to produce sufficient insulin. It is characterised by uncontrolled hig blood glucose levels and is normally treated with regular insulin injections.
- In Type 2 diabetes, the body cells no longer respond to the insu produced by the pancreas. A carbohydrate-controlled diet and exercise regime are common treatments. Obesity is a major risk factor for Type 2 diabetes.

Water balance 4.5.3

- If body cells gain or lose too much water by osmosis, they do n function efficiently.
  - If body fluids become too dilute, cells can swell and burst as they take up more water by osmosis.
  - If body fluids are too concentrated, cells can shrink as more water leaves by osmosis.
- Uncontrollable water loss:
  - Via the lungs during exhalation.
  - Water, ions and urea are lost from the skin in sweat.
- The controlled removal of excess water (to maintain water balance), ions and urea takes place in the kidneys, which produ urine and maintain the water balance.

Protein removal 4.5.3

- The digestion of proteins from the diet results in excess amino acids, which need to be excreted safely.
- In the liver, excess amino acids are deaminated to form ammon
- Ammonia is toxic so it is immediately converted into urea.
- Urea in cells move into the blood plasma and travel to the kidn for excretion.

The kidney 4.5.3

- The kidneys produce urine by filtration of the blood and selecti reabsorption of useful substances, such as glucose, water and some ions.
- The water balance in the body is controlled by the hormone AD
  - ADH is released by the pituitary gland when the blood is too concentrated.
  - ADH increases the permeability of the kidney tubules.
  - This causes more water to be reabsorbed back into the bloo from the kidney tubules.
  - This is an example of control by negative feedback as more ADH is released when the blood is more concentrated.

Hormones in human reproduction

Kidney failure 4.5.3.3

Kidney failure happens when a person's kidneys are no longer able to filter their blood effectively and can lead to toxicity.

Kidney dialysis can be used to treat kidney failure temporarily by the removal of high levels of urea.

- The blood is filtered out of the body through a dialysis machine, an artificial kidney, before being returned to the body.
- The blood flows past dialysis fluid, which is separated from it by a partially permeable membrane and contains no urea, but the same concentration of glucose and ions.
- Urea diffuses from the highly-concentrated blood into the dialysis fluid with a lower concentration.
- Dialysis takes several hours and must happen several times a week.

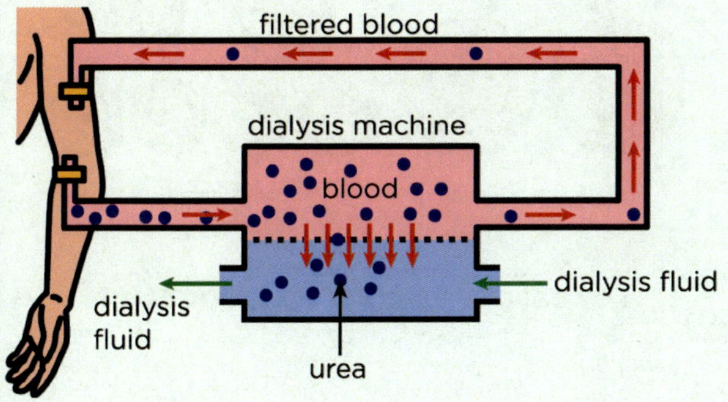

An organ transplant can be used to treat kidney failure.

- Humans have two kidneys and only require one to survive. Hence, a living person can donate a kidney for transplant.
- The body may treat the kidney as foreign and the body's immune system may attack it.
- Immunosuppressant drugs are given to the patient to reduce the chances of rejection; however, these weaken their immune system.
- To minimise the chance of rejection, many donated kidneys come from close family members.
- Tissue typing can be used to determine whether or not a kidney is likely to be rejected.
- The operation is a permanent cure for kidney failure.

Hormones in reproduction 4.5.3.4

During puberty, reproductive hormones cause secondary sex characteristics to develop, e.g. growth of pubic hair.

Oestrogen is the main female reproductive hormone, which is produced in the ovaries. At puberty, eggs begin to mature, and one is released approximately every 28 days (ovulation).

Testosterone is the main male reproductive hormone produced by the testes, which stimulates sperm production.

The menstrual cycle 4.5.3.4

- The menstrual cycle is around 28 days long.
- It requires oestrogen and progesterone from the ovaries and follicle-stimulating hormone (FSH) and luteinising hormone (LH) produced by the pituitary gland.
- Several hormones interact in the menstrual cycle to control it:
  - Follicle-stimulating hormone (FSH) causes maturation of an egg in the ovary and stimulates ovaries to produce oestrogen.
  - Oestrogen is responsible for thickening the uterus lining in preparation for a fertilised ovum, after menstruation.
  - High oestrogen concentration inhibits the release of FSH and stimulates the release of LH.
  - Luteinising hormone (LH) stimulates the release of the egg around day 14.
  - Progesterone maintains the thick uterus lining if a fertilised ovum embeds in it, preventing menstruation.
  - High progesterone concentration inhibits the release of FSH and LH.
  - If no fertilised ovum embeds in the uterus lining, less progesterone is produced, and the uterus lining shreds (menstruation). This starts on day 1, lasts approximately 5 days, and marks the start of the cycle.

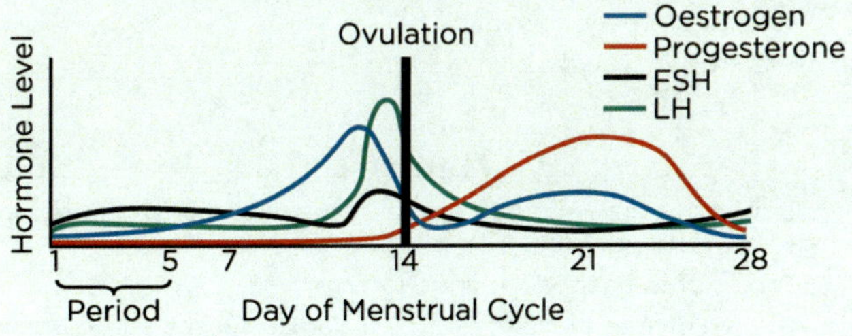

Infertility 4.5.3.6

- FSH and LH can be artificially provided in fertility drugs to support natural pregnancy through sexual intercourse.
- In Vitro Fertilisation (IVF) treatment:
  - FSH and LH are given to stimulate the maturation of several eggs.
  - The eggs are collected and fertilised by sperm in vitro (outside the body) in a laboratory.
  - The fertilised eggs develop into embryos.
  - When the embryos are a tiny ball of cells, one or two embryos are inserted into the uterus to develop.
- Fertility treatments allow people to have babies who otherwise might not be able to.
- Disadvantages of fertility treatment:
  - It is emotionally and physically stressful.
  - Low success rates.
  - It can lead to multiple births, which are a risk to both the babies and the person giving birth.
  - What happens to the unused fertilised embryos can be considered an ethical decision.

Contraception 4.5.3.5

- Fertility can be controlled by a variety of hormonal and non-hormonal methods of contraception.

Non-hormonal method	Description
Barrier method, e.g. condoms, femidoms, contraceptive sponges, diaphragms	Prevent the sperm from reaching an egg
Spermicidal agents	Often found coating barrier methods to kill or disable sperm
Intrauterine devices	Prevent implantation of an embryo
Abstaining from intercourse, especially during ovulation	No sperm enters the female reproductive system
Surgical methods of sterilisation	Vasectomy: sperm ducts are tied or cut Tubal ligation: fallopian tubes are tied or cut

Hormonal method	Description
Oral contraceptives	• Contain oestrogen and progesterone to inhibit FSH production so that no eggs mature • Thicken mucus in the neck of the uterus so it is harder for sperm to travel through • Thin the lining of the uterus so there is less chance of a fertilised ovum embedding
Injection, implant, or skin patch	Slow-release progesterone to inhibit the maturation and release of eggs over several months or years
Intrauterine devices	Release progesterone to prevent implantation

Hormones and cellular reproduction

Adrenaline 4.5.3.7

- Adrenaline is produced by the adrenal glands in times of fear or stress, preparing the body for 'flight or fight':
  - Increases heart rate, blood pressure, and blood glucose levels, boosting the delivery of oxygen and glucose to the brain and muscles for respiration.
  - Suppresses immune system.
  - Levels are not controlled by negative feedback.

Thyroxine 4.5.3.7

- Thyroxine is produced by the thyroid gland:
  - Stimulates the basal metabolic rate.
  - Plays an important role in growth and development.
  - Levels are controlled by negative feedback, maintaining the levels within certain limits.

Tropisms 4.5.4.1

- Plants produce hormones called auxins to coordinate and control growth in response to light (phototropism) and gravity (gravitropism or geotropism).
- Auxins are produced in the tips of shoots and roots.
- Unequal distributions of auxin cause unequal growth rates in plant roots and shoots.
- **Phototropism**:
  - Plant shoots grow towards the light (positive phototropism) to maximise the light absorbed for photosynthesis.
  - In shoots, auxin causes cell elongation.
  - Auxins will concentrate on the shaded side of the shoot, causing unequal growth that makes the shoot bend towards the light.
- **Gravitropism**:
  - Plant roots grow downwards towards water (positive geotropism) in response to gravity, while plant shoots are negatively gravitropic.
  - In roots, auxin slows cell growth on the lower side, causing curvature downwards.

Other plant hormones 4.5.4.1

- Gibberellins:
  - Involved in plant growth.
  - Initiate seed germination and stem elongation.
  - Form flowers and fruit.
- Ethene:
  - Causes the ripening of fruit.
  - Controls cell division.
  - Involved in the opening of flowers and dropping of leaves.

Uses of plant hormones 4.5.4.2

- Plant growth hormones are used in agriculture and horticulture.
- Auxins:
  - Selective weed killers – broad-leaved weeds, such as dandelions, have a larger surface area to absorb more weed killer, which causes uncontrollable growth of some cells and inhibits growth in others, killing the plant.
  - Rooting powders – plant cuttings are taken, and the cut end of the stem is dipped in rooting powder and placed into the soil where auxin helps the cutting form roots.
  - Auxins are used to promote growth in tissue culture.
- Ethene:
  - Ethene is used to control the ripening of fruit.
  - Fruit is often picked before it is ripe to prevent rotting during the long journey to supermarkets.
  - Ethene is sprayed on fruit before arriving so it begins to ripen as it is placed on the shelves.
- Gibberellins:
  - Used to end seed dormancy to trigger germination.
  - Used to promote flowering.
  - Used to increase the size of fruit.

Meiosis 4.6.1.2

- Cells in reproductive organs divide by meiosis to form gametes, halving the number of chromosomes:
  - Copies of the genetic information are made.
  - The cell divides twice to form four gametes, each with a single set of chromosomes.
  - All gametes are genetically different from each other.
- Gametes fuse at fertilisation, forming a zygote and restoring the full number of chromosomes.
- The zygote divides by mitosis, increasing the number of cells to form an embryo.
- The cells differentiate as the embryo develops.

Sexual reproduction 4.6.1.1

- Meiosis leads to non-identical cells being formed.
- Gametes are formed using meiosis.
- Sexual reproduction involves the fusion of male and female gametes (fertilisation):
  - Sperm and egg cells in animals.
  - Pollen and egg cells in flowering plants.
- There is a mixing of genetic information from each parent, which leads to variety in offspring.

Asexual reproduction 4.6.1

- Asexual reproduction involves only one parent and no fusion of gametes, so there is no mixing of genetic information.
- Mitosis occurs, which produces cells that are genetically identica (clones) to the parent cell.
- Prokaryotic bacteria reproduce asexually.

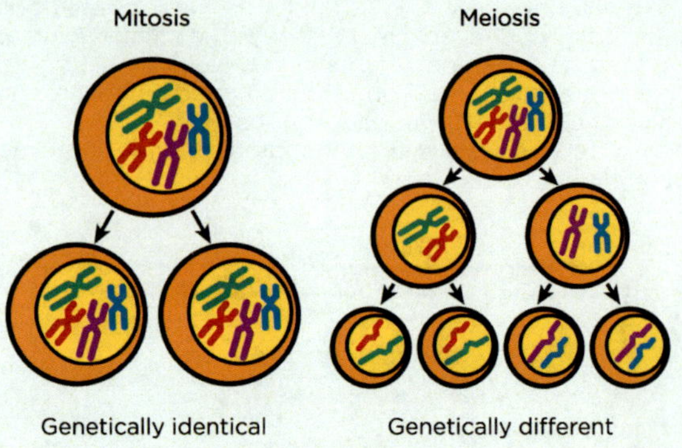

Sexual vs. asexual reproduction 4.6.1

- Some organisms can reproduce by both sexual and asexual reproduction:
  - Malarial parasites reproduce asexually in the human host and sexually in the mosquito.
  - Many fungi can reproduce asexually by spores and sexually tc give variation.
  - Many plants produce seeds sexually but can also reproduce asexually, e.g. runners in strawberry plants or bulb division in daffodils.

	Advantages
Sexual reproduction	• Produces genetic variation in offspring • If the environment changes, variation gives a survival advantage by natural selection (if there is a change in the environment, some organisms may survive due to adaptations) • Natural selection can be sped up by humans through selective breeding (e.g. breeding the best plants to increase food production)
Asexual reproduction	• Only one parent needed • More time and energy-efficient as individuals do not need to find a mate • Faster than sexual reproduction • Many identical offspring can be produced in favourable conditions

SNAPREVISE

DNA structure 4.6.1.5

DNA is a long polymer made from repeating nucleotide units consisting of alternating sugar and phosphate groups with the sugar attached to one of four bases.

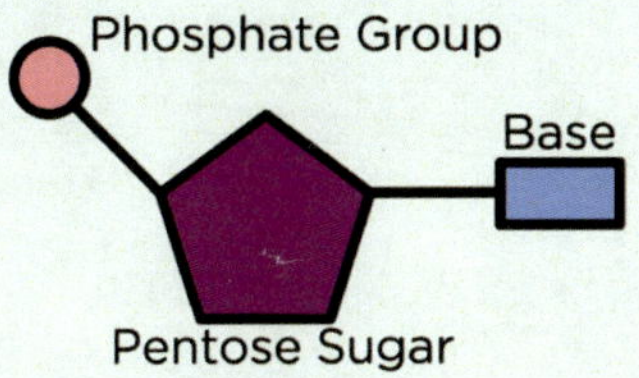

Nucleotide

DNA contains four different bases: A, C, G, and T.

A sequence of three bases is the code for a particular amino acid, so the order determines the assembly of proteins.

Two DNA strands form a double helix.

The strands are complementary (the bases are the correct shape to bind to a specific base on the opposite strand via hydrogen bonds):

- C always binds to a G.
- T always binds to an A.

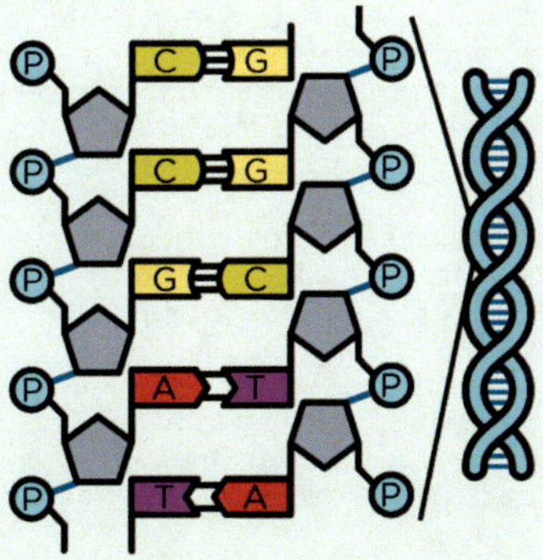

Uses of the Human Genome Project 4.6.1.4

In the Human Genome Project, the sequence of all the bases in the entire human genome was identified using the DNA of male and female volunteers.

Advantages of sequencing the human genome:

- To link genes to different types of diseases.
- To improve our understanding and treatment of inherited disorders
- To trace human migration patterns from the past.

DNA 4.6.1.4

- The genetic material in the nucleus of a cell is made up of a chemical called DNA.
  - DNA is a polymer made up of two strands forming a double helix.
  - The DNA is contained in structures called chromosomes.
  - A gene is a small section of DNA on a chromosome.
  - Each gene codes for a sequence of amino acids that makes a specific protein.
- The genome is the entire genetic material of an organism.

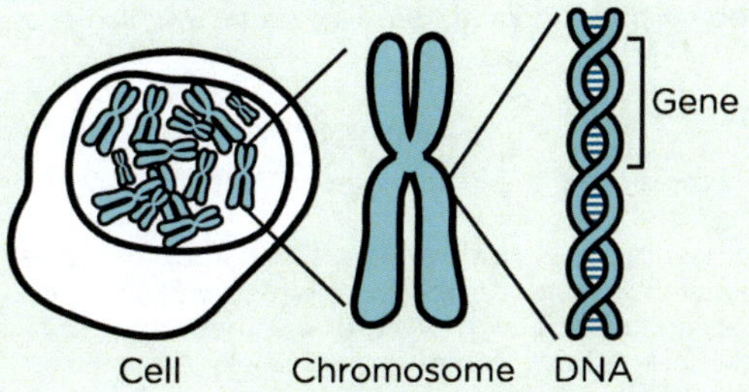

Transcription 4.6.1.5

- Transcription is the first stage of protein synthesis and takes place in the nucleus.
- An mRNA template is formed from a section of one of the nucleotide strands making up DNA.
- The template formed covers a section of DNA that codes for a particular protein (a gene).

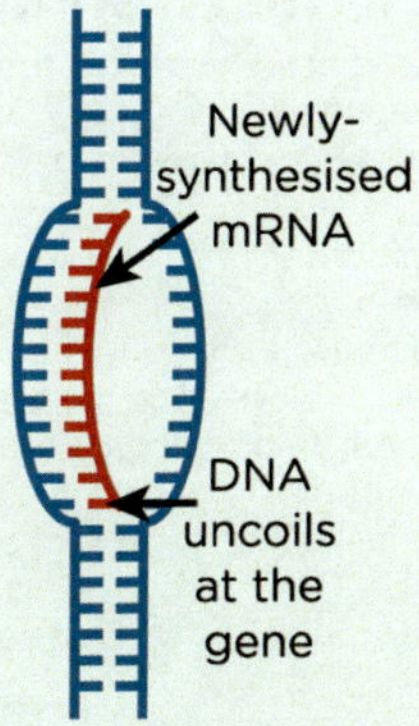

Translation 4.6.1.5

- Translation is the second stage of protein synthesis and takes place on ribosomes.
- tRNA carrier molecules bring amino acids that are specific to the template.
- A sequence of three bases on the template is the code for an amino acid. Therefore, the order of bases controls the order in which the amino acids are assembled and determines the protein that is made.
- The amino acids brought to the template bind to each other, forming a growing protein chain in the correct order.
- When the protein chain is complete, it folds up to form a unique shape.
- The shape of a protein enables it to do its job as an enzyme or hormone or allows it to form a structure in the body, e.g. collagen.

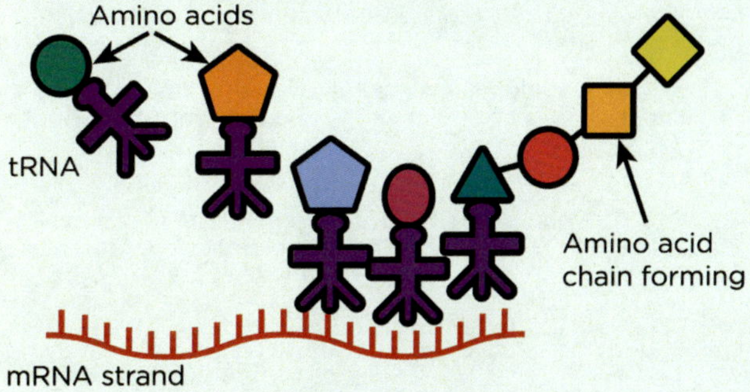

Mutations 4.6.1.5

- A mutation is a change in the DNA sequence; for example, an insertion of a nucleotide or a deletion of one.
- Mutations occur continuously.
- Most mutations do not alter the protein or only alter it slightly so that its shape and therefore function is not changed.
- A few mutations code for an altered protein with a different shape, altering the activity of a protein, e.g. an enzyme may no longer fit the substrate-binding site or a structural protein may lose its strength.
- Some mutations are advantageous and allow genetic variation.

Gene expression 4.6.1.5

- Not all parts of DNA code for proteins.
- Non-coding parts of DNA play a role in gene expression and can switch genes on and off.
- Variations in non-coding regions may affect how genes are expressed.

Inheritance and variation

Inheritance and alleles 4.6.1.6

Term	Definition
Gamete	Sex cells that contain half the number of chromosomes of all other cells with male and female gametes combining in fertilisation
Chromosome	Structures of DNA found in the nucleus of eukaryotic cells
Gene	A section of DNA that codes for a particular protein
Allele	Alleles are two versions of the same gene
Dominant	A dominant allele is always expressed. Will show a characteristic if inherited from one or both parents
Recessive	Allele will only be expressed and show a characteristic if two copies are present, one from each parent
Homozygous	A genotype with two of the same alleles
Heterozygous	A genotype with two different alleles
Genotype	The collection of genes/alleles present in an organism
Phenotype	The physical characteristics of an organism, determined by the genotype and environment

- Some characteristics are controlled by a single gene:
  - Fur colour in mice.
  - Red-green colour blindness in humans.
- Most characteristics are a result of the interaction of multiple genes, rather than a single gene.

Phenotype and genotype 4.6.1.6

- 'B' is the brown eye allele. It is capitalised to signify it is dominant. If someone has a 'B' in their genotype, they will have brown eyes (Bb or BB).
- 'b' is the blue eye allele. It is lower case to signify it is recessive. Both alleles must be 'b' in someone's genotype for them to have blue eyes (bb only).
- If the genotype is 'BB', the phenotype would be 'brown eyes'.

Punnett squares 4.6.1.6

- A Punnett square is a grid used to determine the probability of an offspring's genotype based on the genotype of the parents.
- It shows the potential allele combinations offspring can inherit.
- Determining the inheritance of eye colour:
  - Both parents have the brown eye phenotype and the genotype Bb.
  - Punnett square:

		Parent 1	
		B	b
Parent 2	B	BB	Bb
	b	Bb	bb

  - Genotype ratio BB:Bb:bb = 1:2:1
  - Probability of offspring: BB = 25%, Bb = 50%, bb = 25%
  - Probability of offspring: Brown eyes = 75%, blue eyes 25%

Family trees 4.6.1.6

- Family trees show the inheritance of characteristics over several generations.
- The oldest members of a family are at the top of a tree.
- People with XY chromosomes are typically symbolised with squares and people with XX chromosomes are symbolised with circles, unless shown otherwise with a key.
- Individuals with a specific characteristic are symbolised by their shape being coloured in, unless shown otherwise with a key.

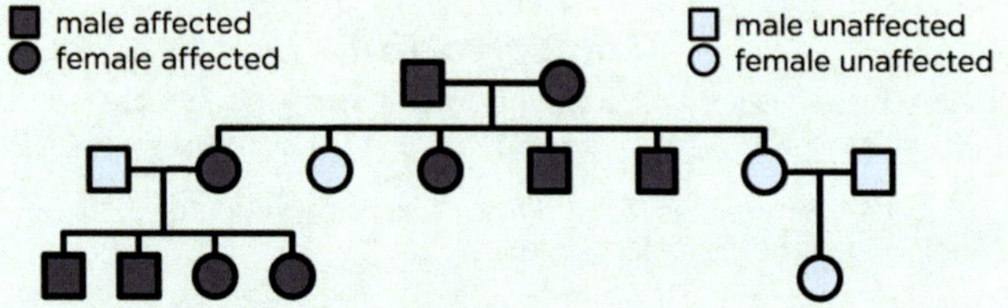

Inherited disorders 4.6.1.7

- Some disorders are inherited, meaning they are caused by the inheritance of certain alleles.
  - Polydactyly (having extra fingers or toes) is caused by a dominant allele.
  - Cystic fibrosis (a disorder of cell membranes) is caused by a recessive allele.
- Embryo screening involves looking for genetic disorders in embryos before they develop, allowing the parents to make an informed decision about continuing or terminating the pregnancy, which may alleviate suffering.
  - There is a possible risk to the embryo, and the person carrying the embryo.
  - It can be seen as unethical or against some religions.
  - It is expensive.

Determining sex 4.6.1.

- Ordinary human body cells contain 23 pairs of chromosomes.
- 22 pairs control characteristics.
- 1 pair carries the genes that determine sex.
  - In females, the sex chromosomes are the same (XX).
  - In males, the sex chromosomes are different (XY).
- Determining the inheritance of sex:
  - Punnett square:

		Mother	
		X	X
Father	X	XX	XX
	Y	XY	XY

  - Genotype ratio XX:XY = 1:1
  - Probability of offspring: XX = 50%, XY = 50%

Variation 4.6.2

- Differences in the characteristics of individuals in a population a called variation.
- The phenotype of an organism is determined by the genome an the genome's interaction with the environment.
  - Some characteristics are determined purely from inherited genes (e.g. biological sex and blood group).
  - Some characteristics are determined purely by the environment (e.g. tattoos and scars).
  - Some characteristics are determined by genetics and the environment, where genetics predetermines the potential for a characteristic and the environment determines how much o this potential is reached (e.g. intelligence).
- There is usually extensive genetic variation within a population c a species.
- All genetic variation arises from mutations:
  - Most mutations have no effect on the phenotype.
  - Some mutations influence phenotype.
  - Very few mutations determine phenotype.
- Mutations occur continuously:
  - Very rarely a mutation will lead to a new phenotype.
  - If the new phenotype is better suited to an environmental change, it can lead to a fairly rapid change in the species.

Evolution 4.6.2.

- The theory of evolution states that all species of living things ha evolved from simple life forms that first developed over 3 billion years ago.
- Evolution is a change in the inherited characteristics of a population over time through a process called natural selection.
- Natural selection of variants in a population gives rise to phenotypes best suited to their environment.
- Natural selection may result in the formation of new species.
- If two populations of a species become so different from each other in phenotype that they can no longer interbreed to produc fertile offspring, they have formed two new species.

Selective breeding 4.6.2.3

Selective breeding (artificial selection) is the process by which humans breed plants and animals for particular genetic characteristics.

Humans have been doing this for thousands of years, e.g. the breeding of food crops from wild plants and the domestication of animals.

Selective breeding involves:

- Choosing parents with a desired characteristic from a mixed population and breeding them together.
- Choosing the offspring with the desired characteristic and breeding them together.
- Repeating the cycle over many generations until all offspring show the desired characteristic.

The characteristic can be chosen for its usefulness or appearance:

- Animals that produce more meat or milk.
- Disease resistance or increased size in food crops.
- Domestic dogs with a gentle nature.
- Large or unusual flowers.

Disadvantages of selective breeding:

- Can lead to 'inbreeding' when the parents are genetically very similar, where some breeds are especially prone to inherited defects or disease.
- Reduced genetic variation means that a change in the environment or a disease is more likely to kill an entire population.
- Physical problems in organisms, e.g. cows weighed down by large udders.
- The breeding method (e.g. artificial insemination) can be seen as unethical.

GM crops 4.6.2.4

GM stands for 'genetically modified'.

GM crops generally show increased yields.

Plant crops have been genetically engineered to:

- Improve resistance to diseases and insect attacks.
- Improve resistance to environmental conditions, e.g. drought.
- Produce bigger and better fruit and vegetables.
- Make crops resistant to the herbicides used on weeds.

Concerns of GM crops:

- Fears that the genes might spread into the wild gene pool, e.g. herbicide-resistant weeds.
- Some people are cautious of the effects of eating GM crops on human health.
- A higher yield of GM crops may cause a reduction in wildflowers and the insects that depend on them as a food source.

Genetic engineering 4.6.2.4

- Genetic engineering is a process that involves modifying the genome of an organism by introducing a gene from another organism to give a desired characteristic.
  - Enzymes are used to isolate the required gene by cutting it from the DNA.
  - The gene is inserted into a vector (a bacterial plasmid or virus). If the vector is a bacterial plasmid, the same enzyme is used to cut open the plasmid and a second is used to seal it.
  - The vector is used to insert the gene into the required cells.

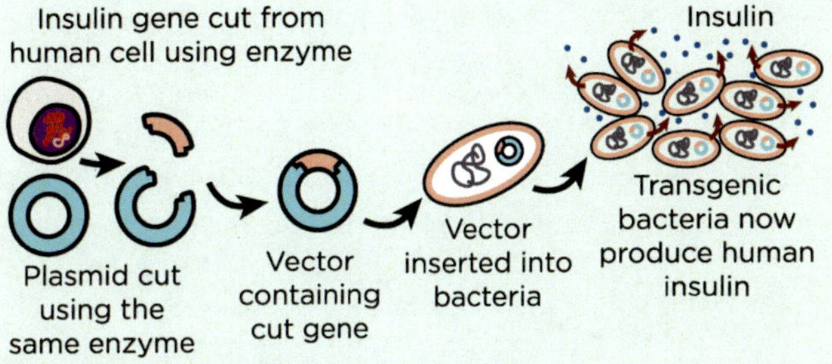

- Genes are transferred to the cells of animals, plants or bacteria at an early stage in their development (e.g. embryo in animals) so they develop with the desired characteristics; all cells produced via mitosis will then contain the same gene.
- Some people disagree with genetic engineering for religious or moral reasons.

GM animals 4.6.2.4

- Animals can be genetically engineered to produce molecules we need.
- Sheep have been genetically engineered to produce proteins used in medicine
- Modern medical research is exploring the possibility of genetic modification to overcome some inherited disorders.

GM bacteria 4.6.2.4

- Bacterial cells have been genetically engineered to produce useful substances, such as human insulin to treat diabetes.
- Benefits:
  - Produces insulin at a high yield.
  - Produces human insulin, which is safer to use than pig or cattle insulin.
- Some people are cautious of the effects of using GM medicines on human health.

Cloning 4.6.2.5

- Cloning is the asexual reproduction of an organism to produce genetically identical offspring, or the artificial cloning of an organism to produce a genetically identical organism.
- Plant cloning is used to grow identical new plants:

Method	Description
Tissue culture	• Takes small groups of cells from part of a plant and places them in a growth medium to grow identical new plants. • Used commercially in nurseries or to preserve rare plant species.
Cuttings	• Older and simpler method used by gardeners. • Cuttings are treated with plant hormones and placed directly into the soil where they develop roots.

- Animal cloning via embryo transplants:
  - Cells from a developing embryo are taken before they become specialised.
  - The cells are split from each other and transplanted into the wombs of multiple host animals.
  - The separated cells develop into identical embryos, forming multiple identical offspring.
  - This is illegal in humans.

Adult cell cloning 4.6.2.5

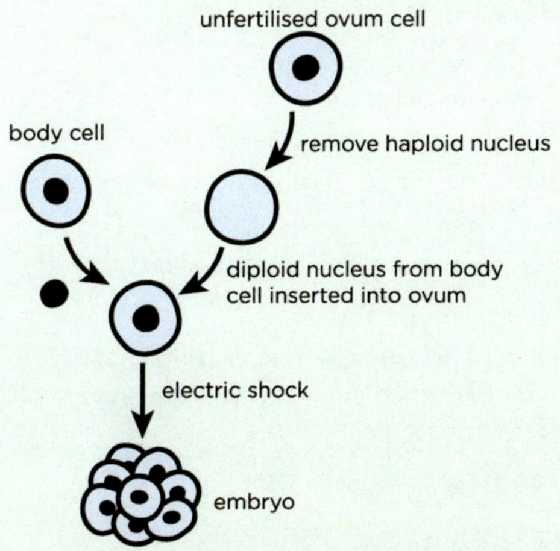

- Adult body cells, such as skin cells, are used.
- When the embryo is a ball of cells, it is inserted into the womb of an adult animal to continue its development.
- The embryo contains the same genetic information as the adult body cell whose nucleus was inserted into the ovum.

Evolution, Mendelian genetics, and extinction

Theory of evolution 4.6.3.1

- Charles Darwin proposed his theory of evolution by natural selection based on:
  - Observations he made on a round-the-world expedition.
  - Developing knowledge of geology and fossils.
- Darwin published his theory in *On the Origin of Species* (1859).
- There was a lot of controversy about his theory.
  - The theory challenged the idea that God made all animals and plants that live on Earth.
  - There was insufficient evidence at the time the theory was published.
  - The mechanism of inheritance and variation was not known until 50 years after the theory was published.
- Jean-Baptiste Lamarck proposed an earlier theory of evolution:
  - Changes that occur in an organism during its lifetime can be inherited.
  - We know that in the vast majority of cases this type of inheritance cannot occur.

Natural selection 4.6.3.1

- The theory of evolution by natural selection:
  - Individual organisms in a species have a wide range of variation for a characteristic.
  - Individuals with characteristics most suited to their environment are more likely to survive long enough to breed successfully.
  - The characteristics that have enabled these individuals to survive are passed onto their offspring.
  - The cycle continues from one generation to the next.

Evidence for evolution 4.6.3.4

- Evidence for Darwin's theory of evolution by natural selection:
  - It has been shown that characteristics are passed on to offspring in genes.
  - Fossil records.
  - Antibiotic resistance has evolved in bacteria.
- Because of this evidence, the theory of evolution by natural selection is now widely accepted.

Fossils 4.6.3.5

- Fossils are the 'remains' of organisms from millions of years ago, which are found in rocks.
- Fossils show us how much or how little different organisms have changed as life developed on Earth, providing evidence for Darwin's theory of evolution by natural selection.
- Fossils may be formed:
  - From parts of organisms that have not decayed because one or more of the conditions needed for decay are absent (e.g. warmth, air, and moisture).
  - When parts of the organism are replaced by minerals as they decay.
  - As preserved traces of organisms, such as footprints, burrows, and rootlet traces.
- Scientists cannot be certain about how life began on earth.
  - Many early forms of life were soft-bodied, meaning that they have left few traces behind.
  - The traces that have been left behind have mainly been destroyed by geological activity over time.

Speciation 4.6.3.2

- Though Darwin is more widely appreciated, Alfred Russel Wallace independently proposed a theory of evolution by natural selection as well.
  - He published joint writings with Darwin in 1858.
  - This prompted Darwin to publish *On the Origins of Species* in 1859.
  - Wallace worked worldwide gathering evidence for evolutionary theory.
- He is best known for his pioneering theory of speciation and his work on warning colouration in animals.
- More evidence over time has led to our current understanding of the theory of speciation, the gradual formation of a new species as a result of evolution.
  - A population of a species is isolated in a different environment to the rest of the species.
  - Different characteristics will be favourable for the survival of individuals in the isolated population as they are in a different environment to the rest of the species.
  - The isolated population will evolve different characteristics to the rest of the species thanks to natural selection.
  - Over time, the isolated population becomes so different from the rest of the species that they can no longer interbreed to form fertile offspring.
  - The isolated population has formed its own species.

Mendelian genetics 4.6.3.

- In the mid-19th century, Gregor Mendel carried out breeding experiments on plants.
- He observed that the inheritance of each characteristic was determined by 'units' that were passed on to the descendants unchanged.
  - Mendel studied the inheritance of traits in pea plants to form the laws of Mendelian inheritance.
  - For example, crossing a yellow pea plant with a green pea plant always produced a yellow pea plant, so yellow was foun to be dominant and green is recessive.
  - These laws are followed when we carry out Punnett squares t determine the potential genotypes of offspring.
- The importance of Mendel's work was not recognised until after his death as little was known about genetic information when his discovery was made; most scientists still believed in blended inheritance, where all characteristics are passed on.
  - Late 19th century – chromosome behaviour during cell divisior was first observed.
  - Early 20th century – Chromosomes and Mendel's 'units' observed to behave in similar ways, leading to the idea that th 'units', later known as genes, were located on chromosomes.
  - Mid-20th century - DNA structure and the mechanism of gene function were determined, leading to the development of gen theory.

Extinction 4.6.3.

- Extinctions occur when there are no remaining individuals of a species still alive.
- Species that do not successfully adapt to environmental conditions or lack the genetic variation to survive changes in the environment are more likely to go extinct.
- Factors that may contribute to the extinction of a species:
  - Increasing population of humans increases human impact on the environment.
    - Cutting down rainforests.
    - Building bigger cities and urban areas.
    - Drilling for oil and materials.
  - Natural changes over time, e.g. end of the ice age.
  - Introduction of new predators.

Antibiotic resistance and interdependent organisms

SNAPREVISE

Solving antibiotic resistance 4.6.3.7

Bacteria reproduce at a fast rate, which means they can evolve rapidly.

- Mutations of bacterial pathogens produce new strains.
- Some strains might be resistant to antibiotics, so they are not killed.
- The resistant strains survive and reproduce, increasing the population of resistant strains.
- The resistant strain is more likely to spread because of the lack of immunity and of an effective treatment.
- For example, MRSA is resistant to antibiotics.

To reduce the rate of development of antibiotic-resistant strains:

- Doctors should not prescribe antibiotics inappropriately, such as treating non-serious or viral infections.
- Patients should always complete their course of antibiotics so that all bacteria are killed and none survive to mutate and form resistant strains.
- The agricultural use of antibiotics should be restricted.

The development of new antibiotics is slow and costly. It is unlikely to keep up with the emergence of new resistant strains.

Classification and Linnaeus 4.6.4

Traditionally living things have been classified into groups depending on their structure and characteristics.
This system was developed by Carl Linnaeus.

- Linnaeus classified living things into kingdom, phylum, class, order, family, genus, and species.
- Organisms are named by the two-part binomial system of genus plus species.
- Scientists write binomial names in italics with a capital letter for the genus, e.g. for the organism *Homo sapiens*, Homo is the genus and sapiens is the species.

Evolutionary trees 4.6.4

Evolutionary trees are a method used by scientists to show how they believe organisms are related.
Evolutionary trees use current classification data for living organisms and fossil data for extinct organisms

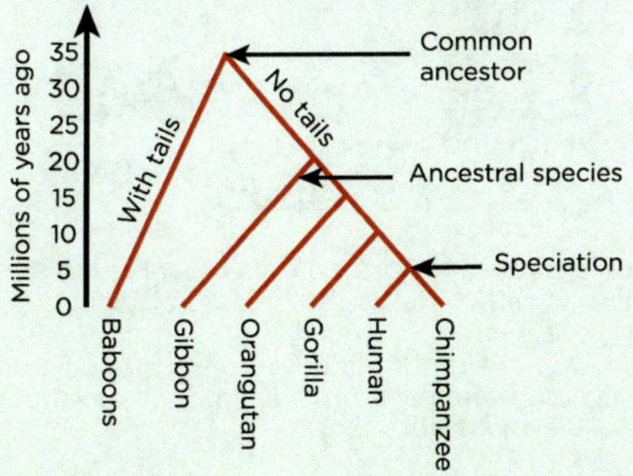

Updates to classification 4.6.4

- New models of classification have been proposed due to:
  - Developing evidence of internal structures due to improvements in microscopes.
  - Increased understanding of biochemical processes.
  - Development of techniques such as genome mapping.
- Due to evidence available from chemical analysis, there is now a 'three-domain system' developed by Carl Woese.
- In this system, organisms are divided into:
  - Archaea (primitive bacteria usually living in extreme environments).
  - Bacteria (true bacteria).
  - Eukaryota (including animals, plants, protists, and fungi).

Interdependence 4.7.1.1

- Within a community, each species depends on other species for food, shelter, pollination, seed dispersal, etc.
- A stable community is one where all the species and environmental factors are in balance with each other so that population sizes remain relatively constant.
- If one species is removed or added it can affect the whole community due to interdependence.

Abiotic factors 4.7.1.2

- Abiotic (non-living) factors that can affect a community are:
  - Light intensity – e.g. plants adapted to the shade may quickly wilt and die if they are moved into direct sunlight.
  - Temperature – e.g. some organisms (e.g. reptiles) cannot regulate their own body temperature.
  - Moisture levels.
  - Soil pH and mineral content.
  - Wind intensity and direction.
  - Carbon dioxide levels for plants – a major limiting factor in photosynthesis.
  - Oxygen levels for aquatic animals – required for respiration.
- A change in an abiotic factor would affect a community, e.g. cacti are adapted to survive with little water and will die if overwatered, so species that depend on cacti for a habitat or a food resource would then also die.

Competition 4.7.1.1

- An ecosystem is the interaction of a community of living organisms (biotic) with the non-living (abiotic) parts of their environment.
- To survive and reproduce:
  - Organisms require a supply of materials from their surroundings and from the other living organisms there.
  - Organisms are adapted to the conditions in which they live.
- Organisms compete with each other for multiple factors:
  - Plants often compete for light, space, and for water and mineral ions from the soil.
  - Animals often compete for food, mates, and territory.
- Competition between organisms provides a struggle for existence, which drives evolution.
  - Only the organisms best adapted to their environment will survive and reproduce, forming offspring also adapted to their environment.
  - This is known as survival of the fittest.
  - Interspecific competition is between different species in a community.
  - Intraspecific competition is between organisms of the same species.

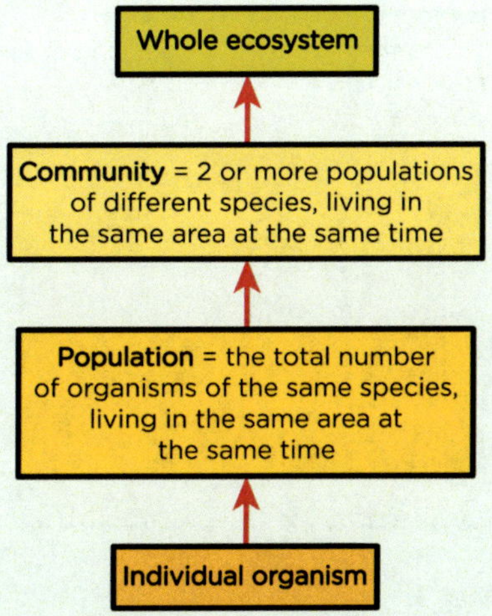

SNAPREVI

Food chains 4.7.2.1

- Feeding relationships within a community can be represented by food chains.

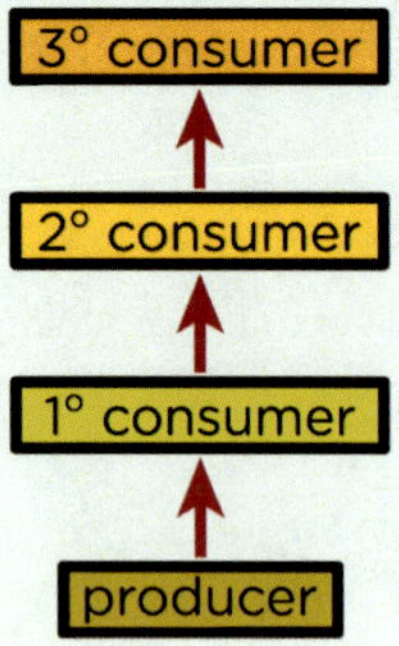

- All food chains begin with a producer, which synthesises molecules.
  - This is usually a green plant or alga.
  - They make glucose by photosynthesis.
  - They are the producers of biomass for life on Earth.
- Producers are eaten by primary consumers, which may be eaten by secondary consumers and then tertiary consumers.
- Predator-prey cycling:
  - Consumers that kill and eat other animals are predators.
  - Consumers that are eaten are prey.
  - In a stable community, the numbers of predators and prey rise and fall in interdependent cycles.
  - If the number of predators increases, the number of prey decrease after a short lag phase, as more are eaten.
  - As the number of prey decrease, the number of predators will decrease as there is less food.
  - This then causes the number of prey to increase, resulting in an increase in predators.

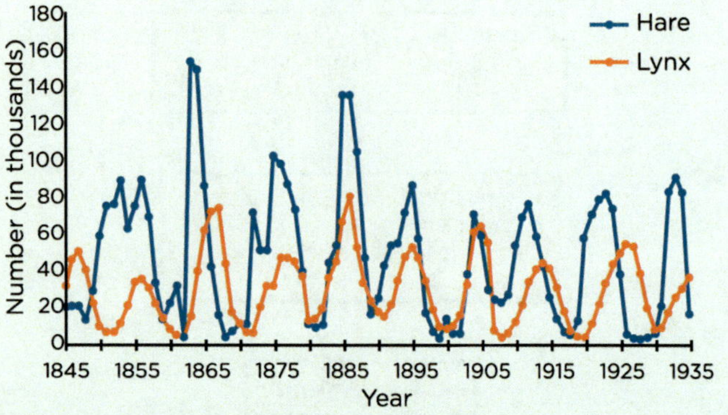

Biotic factors 4.7.1.3

- Biotic (living) factors that can affect a community are:
  - Availability of food.
  - New predators arriving.
  - New pathogens.
  - One species outcompeting another so the numbers are no longer sufficient to breed.
- A change in a biotic factor would affect a community, e.g. if a new pathogen appeared and killed an entire species, the organisms depending on this species for food or a habitat would also die.

Adaptations 4.7.1.4

- Organisms have features called adaptations that enable them to survive in the conditions in which they normally live.
  - Structural adaptations are physical features, e.g. tigers have sharp teeth to allow them to kill their prey.
  - Behavioural adaptations are behaviours that benefit an organism, e.g. a courtship display to attract a mate.
  - Functional adaptations are physiological processes organisms complete to aid survival, e.g. producing venom to deter predators from killing them.
- Adaptations allow organisms to outcompete others and provide them with an evolutionary advantage.
- Organisms called extremophiles live in environments that are very extreme.
  - Extreme conditions include extremely hot or cold temperatures, high pressure or salt concentration, and highly acidic or alkaline environments.
  - For example, bacteria living in deep-sea hydrothermal vents are extremophiles evolved to feed on the sulfur compounds released by the vents, toxic to almost all other life.

Sampling 4.7.2

- Sampling is the process scientists use to look at a section of a habitat and draw conclusions about the whole of it.
- The section of the habitat studied must be large enough to be representative of the whole of it for accurate predictions to be made.
- A range of experimental methods using transects and quadrats are used by ecologists to determine the distribution and abundance of species in an ecosystem.
  - A quadrat is a square frame separated into a grid. It is placed on the ground and the abundance of organisms within square are recorded.
  - A transect is a straight line from one side of the habitat to the other.
  - Distribution and abundance can be determined by systematically recording all the organisms present along a transect, by placing a quadrat at fixed intervals along it.
- Methods of measuring the abundance of organisms:
  - Mode: The value that appears most frequently in a data set.
  - Median: The middle number in a data set when displayed in ascending order
  - $mean\ (average) = \frac{sum\ of\ terms}{number\ of\ terms}$

The carbon cycle 4.7.2.

- Many different materials cycle through the abiotic and biotic components of an ecosystem.
- All materials in the living world are recycled to provide the building blocks for future organisms
- The carbon cycle is important so that living organisms can continually be supplied with carbon in forms suitable for use in making the molecules necessary for life, e.g. proteins, carbohydrates, lipids and nucleic acids.

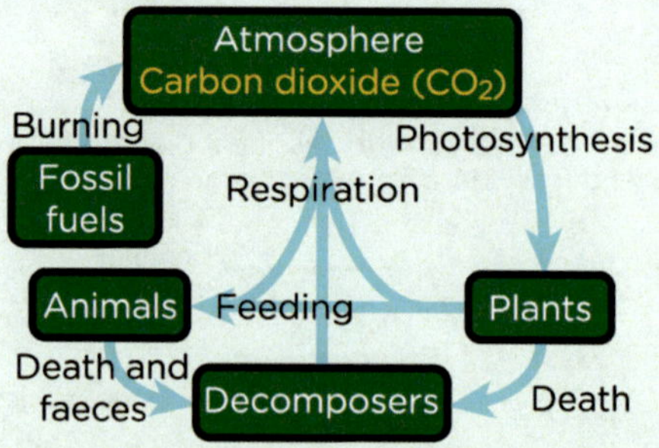

- The carbon cycle returns carbon from organisms to the atmosphere as carbon dioxide to be used by plants in photosynthesis.
- Microorganisms are important decomposers that cycle materials through an ecosystem by returning carbon to the atmosphere as carbon dioxide and mineral ions to the soil.

The water cycle 4.7.2.2

The water cycle is important so that living organisms can continually be supplied with water, which is the major component of all cells and therefore necessary for life.

The water cycle provides fresh water for plants and animals on land before draining into the seas.

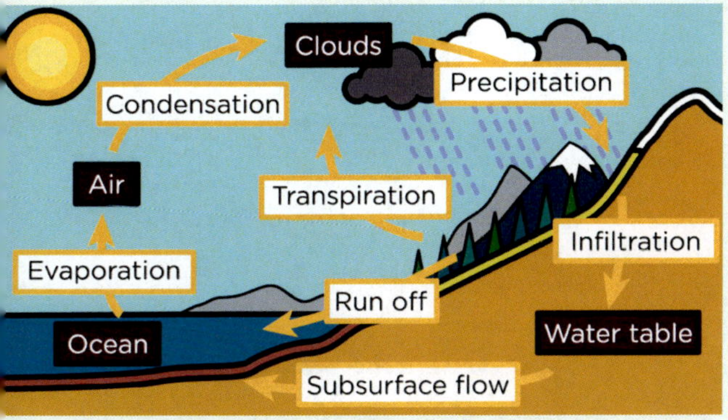

Water is continuously evaporated and precipitated (as rain, snow, hail or sleet).

Runoff is the movement of water across the surface.

Infiltration is the movement of water into the ground to become groundwater.

Subsurface flow is the movement of groundwater to the ocean.

Decomposition 4.7.2.3

Decomposition is the breakdown of substances into smaller substances, carried out by bacteria and fungi.

Increasing temperature, oxygen and water availability increases the rate of decay of biological material as bacteria and fungi grow faster.

$$rate\ change\ in\ the\ decay\ of\ biological\ material = \frac{change\ in\ value}{time}$$

Gardeners and farmers try to provide optimum conditions (e.g. neutral pH) for rapid decay of waste biological material to produce compost.

Compost is used as a natural fertiliser.

Anaerobic decay produces methane gas, which can be carried out in a biogas generator to produce fuel.

Effects of environmental change 4.7.2.4

- Environmental changes affect the distribution of species in an ecosystem.
- These changes may be seasonal, geographic, or caused by human interaction.

Change	Explanation	Example
Temperature	Enzymes have an optimum temperature at which they function.	Seasonal: seasonal decreases in temperature can cause migrations, e.g. towards winter, birds, such as swallows, migrate south from Northern Europe toward hotter temperatures.
Availability of water	No life can exist without water.	Geographic: in deserts, cacti and camels have adapted to survive with minimal water, and most life and green plants are found surrounding oases (where water rises from underground sources). The distribution of algal species also varies depending on the tide.
Composition of atmospheric gases	Combustion of fossil fuels release gases that can be toxic to organisms (e.g. oxides of carbon, sulfur and nitrogen).	Human interaction: most lichens will only grow in high numbers in clear air as they are sensitive to air pollution. The distribution of species can be a useful bioindicator of air pollution.

Biodiversity 4.7.3.1

- Biodiversity is the variety of all the different species of organisms on earth, or within an ecosystem.
- A great biodiversity ensures the stability of ecosystems by reducing the dependence of one species on another for:
  - Food
  - Shelter
  - Maintenance of the physical environment
- The future of the human species on Earth relies on us maintaining a good level of biodiversity.
- Many human activities are reducing biodiversity (e.g. deforestation) and only recently have measures been taken to try to stop this reduction.

Waste management 4.7.3.2

- Increasingly more resources are being used and more waste is being produced due to:
  - Rapid growth in the human population.
  - An increase in the standard of living.
- Unless waste and chemical materials are properly handled, more pollution will be caused.
- Pollution kills plants and animals, which can reduce biodiversity.
- Pollution can occur:
  - In water – from sewage, fertiliser, or toxic chemicals.
  - In air – from smoke and acidic gases.
  - On land – from landfill and toxic chemicals.

Land use 4.7.3.3

- Humans reduce the amount of land available for other animals and plants by building, quarrying, farming, and dumping waste.
- The destruction of peat bogs and other areas of peat may occur to produce garden compost:
  - Peat is made up of partially decayed vegetation.
  - Destruction reduces the area of this habitat and the variety of different species living there (biodiversity).
  - The decay or burning of the peat releases carbon dioxide into the atmosphere.

Deforestation 4.7.3.4

- Large-scale deforestation in tropical areas has occurred to:
  - Provide land for cattle and rice fields.
  - Grow crops for biofuels.
- Environmental implications of deforestation:
  - Increase in carbon dioxide in the atmosphere as there are fewer trees to take in carbon dioxide for photosynthesis.
  - Burning of trees increases atmospheric carbon dioxide.
  - Reduces biodiversity as it destroys species of tree and removes habitat for several species of animals.
  - Causes drier climates as there is less transpiration by trees, resulting in drier soils, fewer roots, and greater risk of erosion and landslides.

Global warming and trophic levels

SNAPREVI

Maintaining biodiversity 4.7.3.6

- Negative effects of humans on ecosystems and biodiversity:
  - Deforestation increases global warming and destroys species' habitats.
  - Burning fossil fuels increases global warming.
  - Industrial processes pollute air and habitats with waste chemicals.
  - Build-up of plastic rubbish in the oceans.
  - Overfishing, which damages wild food chains.
  - Oil spills can kill aquatic organisms and species, such as sea birds, sea otters and seals.
- Scientists and concerned citizens have put in place programmes to reduce the negative effects of humans on ecosystems and biodiversity:
  - Breeding programmes for endangered species to promote reproduction and safeguard the widest possible gene pool to increase the chances of survival of the offspring.
  - Protection and regeneration of rare habitats, such as rainforests.
  - Reintroduction of field margins and hedgerows in agricultural areas where farmers grow only one type of crop, providing habitats for wild species.
  - Reduction of deforestation and carbon dioxide emissions by some governments.
  - Recycling resources rather than dumping waste in landfills.
  - Quotas on fishing.

Trophic levels 4.7.4.1

- A trophic level is a level in a food chain.
- Trophic levels can be represented by numbers according to how far an organism is along the food chain.

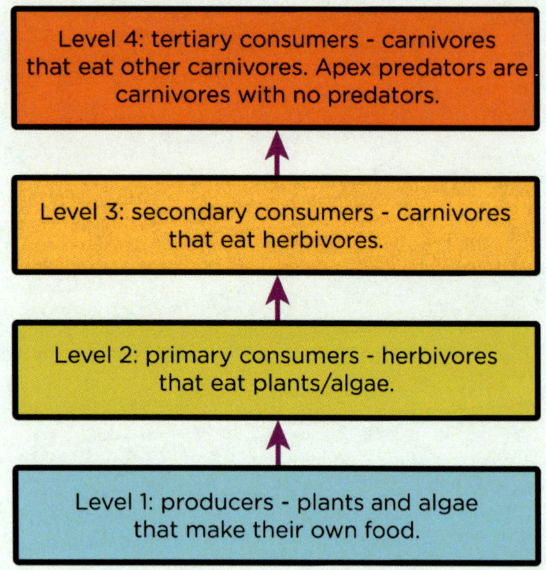

- Decomposers include bacteria, fungi and worms.
  - They break down dead plant and animal matter by secreting enzymes into the environment.
  - Small soluble food molecules then diffuse into the microorganism.
  - This also releases mineral ions and nutrients that plants can absorb from the soil.

Pyramids of biomass 4.7.4

- Biomass is the mass of any living or recently dead organism in grams or kilograms.
- Organisms can gain energy from consuming biomass and turn this energy into their body tissue (their own biomass).
- Dead organisms are first dried in an oven before biomass is recorded as different organisms contain different amounts of water.
- Pyramids of biomass can be constructed to represent the relativ amount of biomass in each level of a food chain.
- Trophic level 1 is at the bottom of the pyramid.

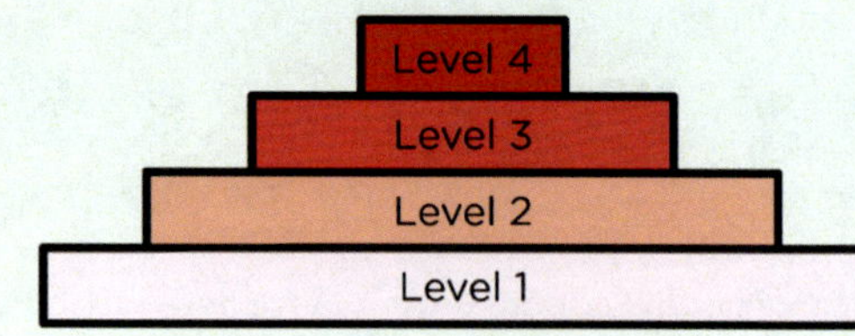

Global warming 4.7.3

- Global warming is the increase in the average temperature of th Earth.
- Levels of carbon dioxide and methane (greenhouse gases) in th atmosphere are increasing and contribute to global warming by trapping more heat.
- The increased emission of greenhouse gases in recent years is due to human activity, e.g. fossil fuel combustion.
- Biological consequences of global warming:
  - Glaciers are melting in the arctic, causing sea levels to rise an a loss of coastal regions and some islands.
  - Loss of suitable habitats for species, causing decreased biodiversity and decreased food security for humans.
  - Extreme weather conditions, e.g. flash floods and droughts.
  - Species are migrating as current conditions are no longer suitable for them.

SNAPREVISE

Transfer of biomass 4.7.4.3

A pyramid of biomass is largest at the bottom and decreases as we go up the levels as biomass is lost between the different trophic levels.

- Not all ingested material is absorbed, some is egested as faeces.
- A lot of absorbed material is lost as waste, such as carbon dioxide and water in respiration and water and urea in urine.
- Large amounts of glucose are used in respiration.

$$Efficiency\ of\ biomass\ transfers = \frac{biomass\ in\ higher\ trophic\ level}{biomass\ in\ lower\ trophic\ level} \times 100\%$$

Producers transfer about 1% of the incident energy from light (from the sun) for photosynthesis.

Only approximately 10% of the biomass from each trophic level is transferred to the level above it.

As biomass and energy are lost at each level up the food chain, often the number of organisms decreases from one trophic level to the next.

However, if level 2 was larger than level 1, then the herbivores may eat all of the plants, affecting the food chain.

Sustainable fisheries 4.7.5.3

Fish stocks in the oceans are declining.

It is important to maintain fish stocks at a level where breeding continues, or certain species may disappear in some areas.

Introducing fishing quotas and regulating net sizes play important roles in the conservation of fish stocks at a sustainable level.

Preventing overfishing promotes the recovery of fish stocks.

Farming techniques 4.7.5.2

- The efficiency of food production can be improved by restricting energy transfer from food animals to the environment.
- This can be done through intensive farming to maximise yields by reducing energy use and biomass loss:
  - Limiting movement by having animals packed together in small pens.
  - Controlling the temperature of their surroundings.
  - Some people have ethical objections to some intensive farming methods, for example restricting movement may affect an animal's quality of life.
- Some animals are fed high-protein foods to increase growth.
- Crop rotation can be done, which may provide less encouragement for pests and be less damaging to soil,

Factors affecting food security 4.7.5.1

- Food security is having enough food to feed a population.
- Sustainable methods must be found to feed all people on Earth.
- Biological factors that are threatening food security include:
  - The increasing birth rate in some countries.
  - Changing diets in developed countries means scarce food resources are transported around the world.
  - New pests and pathogens that affect farming.
  - Environmental changes that affect food production, such as widespread famine occurring in some countries if rains fail.
  - The cost of agricultural inputs.
  - Conflicts that have arisen in some parts of the world that affect the availability of water or food.

Biotechnology 4.7.5.4

- Possible biotechnical and agricultural solutions to the demands of the growing human population:

Demand	Solution
Meat substitute for vegetarians	• Modern biotechnology techniques enable large quantities of microorganisms to be cultured for food. • The fungus *Fusarium* is used to produce mycoprotein, a protein-rich food suitable for vegetarians. • The fungus is grown on glucose syrup in aerobic conditions, and the biomass is harvested and purified.
Insulin for diabetics	• Initially, purified pig insulin was used but some people have allergic reactions to it. • Now a genetically modified bacterium produces human insulin, which can be harvested and purified to treat people with diabetes.
More food or food with improved nutritional value	Genetically modified crops, e.g. golden rice, which reduces the chance of vitamin A deficiency.

Scientific processes WS 1.1, 1.6

- Scientific ideas are not accepted until there is evidence to back them up.
  - Theories, theorems and experimental results are published in scientific journals.
  - These undergo peer review by the scientific community before they are accepted.
  - Scientists will also repeat experiments described in journals to confirm their results are valid.
  - Some scientific ideas considered correct today were not initially accepted until decades after they were first published, such as Darwin's theory of evolution.
- Currently accepted scientific theories and models are the ones that best fit the current evidence and knowledge of the universe. They may be disproven at some point in the future.
- Scientific ideas that are reported in popular media before verification can lead to negative opinions of them.
  - These reports are not subject to peer review so they could concern scientific ideas that turn out to be incorrect.
  - There is a risk of inaccuracies and bias in these reports.
  - More scientists are communicating directly with the public to try and stop this miscommunication.

Variables WS 2.2

- Scientific experiments are performed to determine the relationship between two or more variables.
- An independent variable is a variable that is manually changed. An experiment should have only one independent variable.
- A dependent variable is a variable that will change as a result of a change in the independent variable.
- The dependent and independent variables are measured to determine the relationship between them.
- A control variable is a variable that must be kept the same throughout the experiment to make the test fair.
- Changing a control variable will make it unclear if that change or a change in the independent variable is responsible for a change in the dependent variable.

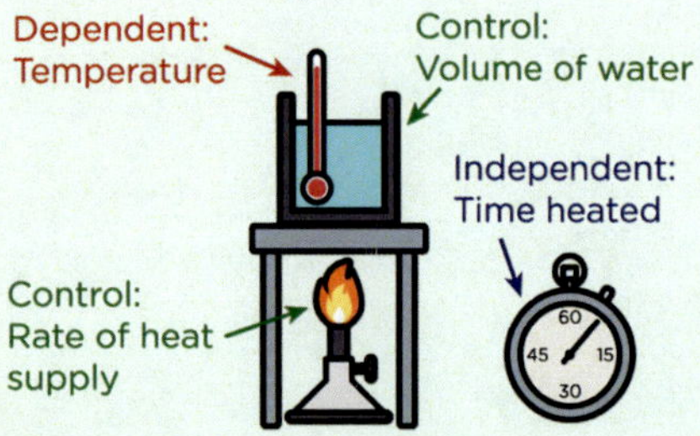

Apparatus and equipment WS 2.2, 2.3

- Diagrams can be used to show how to set up equipment for an experiment. Symbols should be 2D, simple and clear to understand.

Examples of scientific apparatus		
Apparatus	**Use**	**Symbol**
Bunsen burner	To provide a constant flow of heat to a substance.	↑ Heat
Beaker	To store water or other fluids. Other containers, such as canonical flasks, might be used depending on the experiment.	
Test tube	To hold a small amount of liquid. Larger tubes for heating are called boiling tubes.	
Tripod	A stand that a Bunsen burner can be placed under. Gauze can be used to place a beaker on top.	
Clamp stand	A stand that can be used in conjunction with clamps and bosses to suspend test tubes and other equipment in the air.	
Funnel	Used to direct liquid into a test tube or another container.	

- Various equipment can be used to take measurements during experiments. More precise equipment will lead to better results.

Examples of measuring equipment	
Equipment	**Used to measure**
Ruler	Length
Measuring cylinder	Volume
Stopwatch	Time
Thermometer	Temperature
Pan balance/scale	Mass

Safe experiments WS 2

- Measures should be taken to ensure experiments are conducted safely.
- Sensible protective clothing should be worn.
  - Goggles or safety visors to protect the eyes from harmful substances.
  - Lab coats to protect clothing from damage or harmful substances.
  - Gloves when handling hazardous materials.
  - Long hair should be tied back.

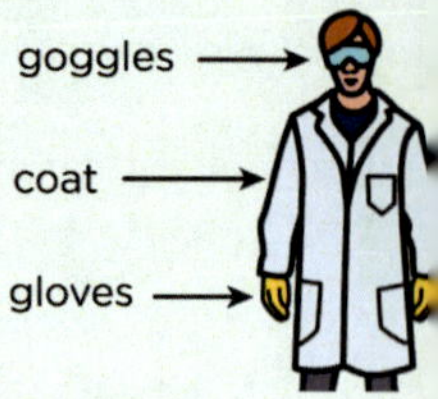

- Steps should be taken to ensure Bunsen burners are used safely.
  - They should always be placed on a heatproof mat.
  - Any heated substances or equipment should be left to cool o only handled with tongs.
  - Bunsen burners should be left on a yellow flame when not in use.
  - Gas taps should be left off when not in use.

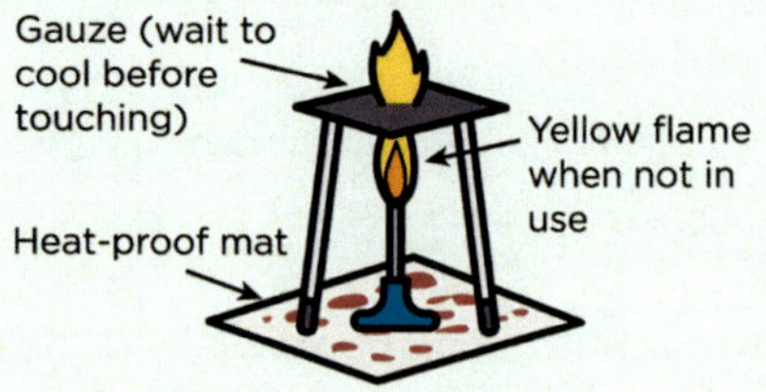

- Hazardous substances, such as chemicals or radioactive materia should be handled with care.
  - They should be stored when not in use.
  - Containers should be correctly marked with the hazards they present (e.g. irritant).
  - Particularly dangerous substances should not be handled directly.
  - Flammable substances should be kept away from naked flam (e.g. ethanol).
- Biohazards, such as bacterial cultures, should be handled with care.
  - Aseptic techniques should be used when preparing bacterial cultures.
  - Disinfectant should be used after exposure to biohazards to prevent contamination.
  - Avoid contact with skin of stains (e.g. Toluidine blue or DCPIP
  - Hands should be washed after handling biohazards or unsterilised samples (e.g. soil samples).
- All equipment should be checked regularly.
  - Clamps and bosses should be tightly secured.
  - Electrical equipment should be inspected to ensure they have no live wires.

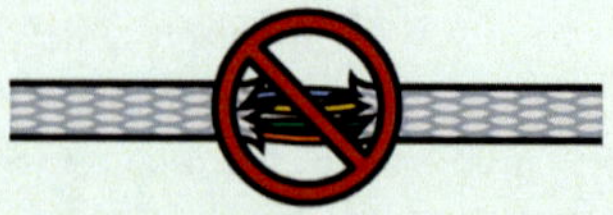

resenting and using data

SNAPREVISE

Presenting data WS 3.1

Frequency tables are used to record results from experiments.
- The first column should be the independent variable with values in increasing order.
- Headers should be clear and include units

Example frequency table

Independent variable, x (s)	Measured variable, y (m)				Calculated dependent variable, y^2 (m^2)
	1	2	3	Mean	
1	1.2	1.4	1.3	1.3	1.7
2	2.8	2.6	3	2.8	7.8
3	3.7	3.2	3.8	3.6	12.7
4	4.8	4.6	4.2	4.5	20.6

Bar charts are used to compare categoric variables to continuous variables.

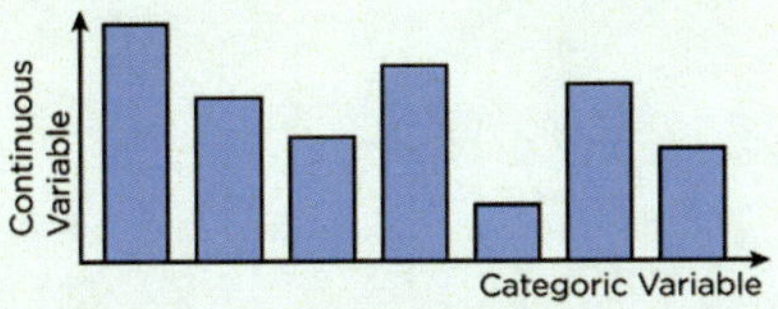

Histograms show how a set of continuous data fits into grouped categories.
- The height of each bar represents the frequency density.
- The area of each bar is proportional to the number of data values in the group.
- The bars should all be touching.

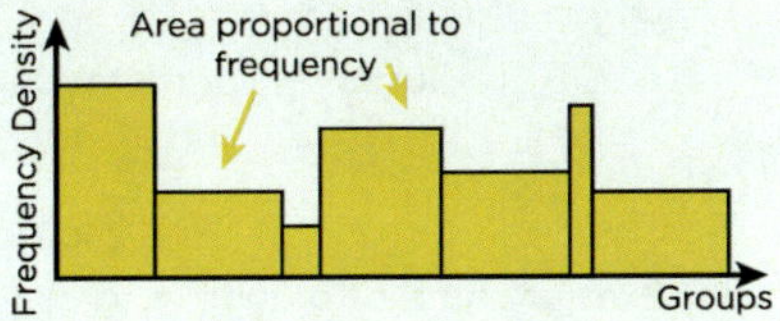

Line graphs compare two continuous variables.
- Recorded data is plotted onto a graph. The x and y coordinates of each point correspond to a value for the independent and dependent variable, respectively.
- A smooth curve is drawn to show the general relationship. This should be close to as many points as possible, excluding outliers.

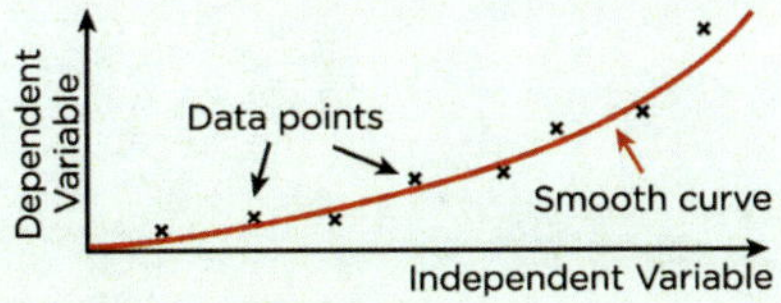

Mean and range WS 3.3

The mean of a set of values is the sum of those values divided by the number of values there are.
- E.g. the mean of **4, 7** and **13** is $(4 + 7 + 13) \div 3 = 8$.
- The mean is used to calculate the average value of the results from a repeated experiment.

The range of the set of values is the difference between the largest and smallest value.
- E.g. the range of the values **4, 7** and **13** is $13 - 4 = 9$.
- The range of a set of measurements can give information about the uncertainty of a repeated experiment.

Rounding and standard form WS 3.3, 4.6

- To round a value to a certain number of significant figures.
  - Identify the first non-zero digit in the value.
  - Count the number of digits after this one.
  - Identify whether to round the last digit in your count up or down, depending on if the next digit is greater than or equal to 5.
  - Remove all digits outside the count.
  - E.g. **0.00548632 = 0.00589** to 3 significant figures.
- Calculated values should be given to a number of significant figures equal to the lowest number of significant figures from the numbers used.
  - E.g. the calculated value **583 × 3.4** should be given to 2 significant figures.
  - Values are rounded to the point where they should be the same as the true value rounded to that many significant figures.
- Standard form is used to write out very large or very small rounded numbers.
  - First, a number between **1** and **10** is written. The number of digits in this number is the same as the number of significant figures it has been rounded to.
  - This is then multiplied by a power of 10, which can be positive or negative depending on if the number is big or small.
  - E.g. $158000 = 1.58 \times 10^5$.
  - E.g. $0.00158 = 1.58 \times 10^{-3}$.
  - Each multiplication by 10 moves the decimal point one digit to the left or right.

Equations WS 3.3

- Equations show the relationship between scientific variables under certain conditions.
- To use an equation to find an unknown value using an equation:
  - Rearrange equation algebraically to make the unknown variable the subject.
  - Substitute in the values in the correct places, ensuring the units are the ones needed for the equation.
  - Calculate the unknown value.
- Formula triangles can be used to help understand how to rearrange equations.
  - Cover the part of the triangle for the unknown value.
  - Divide the top value by the bottom value, or multiply both of the bottom values, depending on which value is unknown.

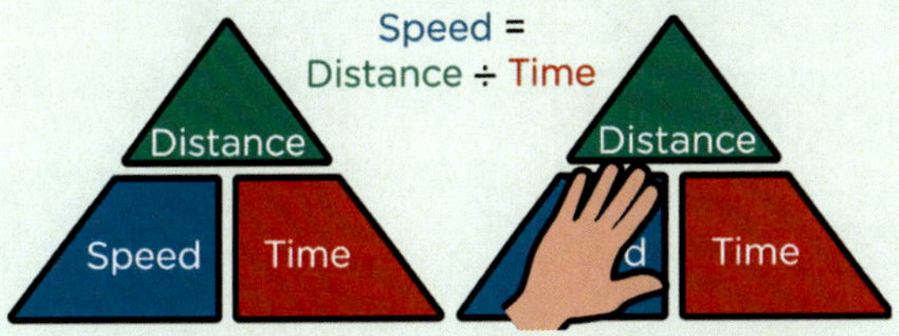

Interpreting graphs WS 1.2, 3.3

- The gradient of a straight line of best fit can give information about the relationship between two variables in a graph.
- To calculate the gradient:
  - Choose two points on the lines as far apart as possible such that their x and y values are easy to read.
  - Calculate the differences in the two x and the two y values.
  - Calculate the gradient as **difference in y ÷ difference in y**.
- A curved line of best fit has a changing gradient. The gradient at a particular point can be calculated by drawing a tangent.
  - A tangent is a straight line that only just brushes against the point on the curve.
  - The gradient of the curve is the gradient of this straight-line tangent.

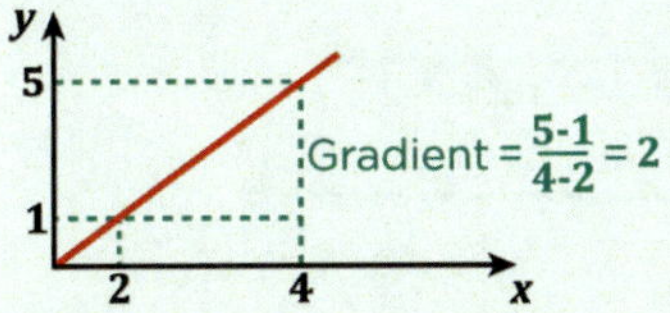

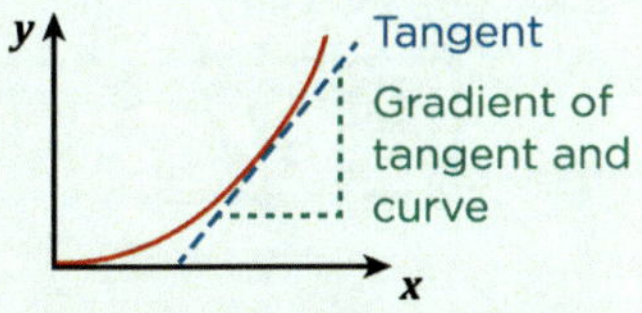

- The x or y intercept is the point where the line crosses the x or y axis.
- The area under a line graph is the value that corresponds to multiplying together the two variables shown in the graph as they are both changing.
  - For straight line graphs, this area can be calculated using the formula for the area of a rectangle or a triangle.
  - For curves, this area can be estimated by counting the squares beneath the graph.

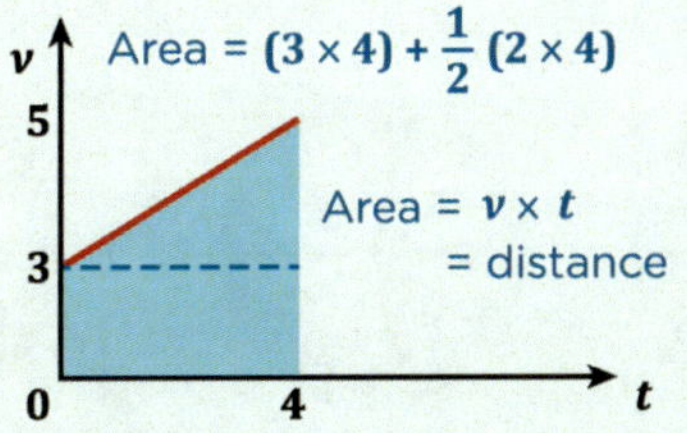

Distance = **52 × 50 m/s × 5s**
= **13000 m**

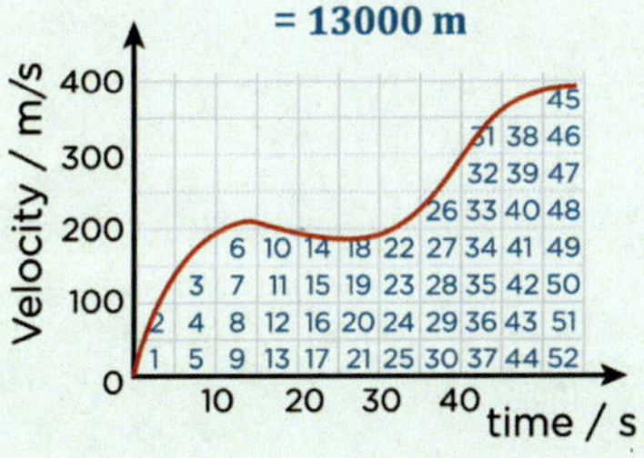

Uncertainty WS 3.4

- Scientific measurements often do not give the true value due to errors. For a repeated experiment, we cannot tell which measurement is closest to the true value.
- The uncertainty of a measurement is the range of values for which it suggests the true value could lie within.
  - Uncertainties are usually given as how far above or below a measured value the true value could be.
  - For example, the value 37.4 ± 2 indicates the true value could be anywhere between 35.4 and 39.4.
- The uncertainty for a repeated experiment can be measured by the range of measurements about the mean. For example, the uncertainty of the measurements $3, 4$ and 5 is 4 ± 1.

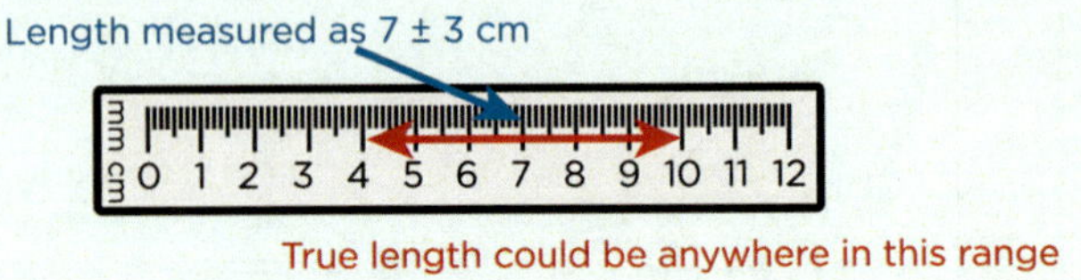

Accuracy and precision WS 3.7

- The true value of a measurement is the value that would be obtained in a perfect experiment without errors.
- The accuracy of a measurement is how close it is to the true value.
- The precision of a repeated experiment is how close together the measurements are.
- Accuracy and precision are two separate concepts. An accurate measurement is not necessarily precise and vice versa.

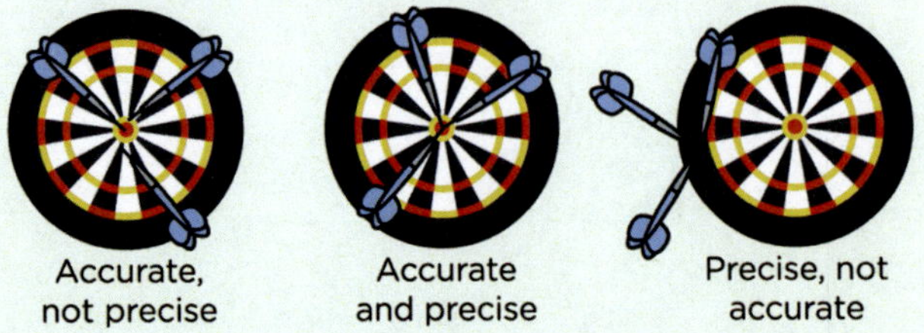

- A measurement is repeatable if the results are similar when the experiment is performed again by the same investigator, under the same conditions. This implies the measurements are precise.
- A measurement is reproducible if the results are similar when the experiment is performed again by a different investigator with different equipment. This implies the measurements are accurate.

Errors and anomalies WS 3.7

- Errors will cause measurements to differ from the true value.
  - Random errors or anomalies affect single experiments and vary unpredictably. This will reduce precision.
  - Systematic errors involve measurement results differing from the true value by a consistent amount each time. This will reduce accuracy.
- Anomalies should be identified and omitted from the results. This can be done by:
  - Repeating experiments to find values that do not match others. For example, in the measurements $3, 7, 25$ and 8, taken under the same conditions, the value 25 would be an anomaly.
  - Plotting results and seeing which values would not fit the pattern established by the rest of the data.

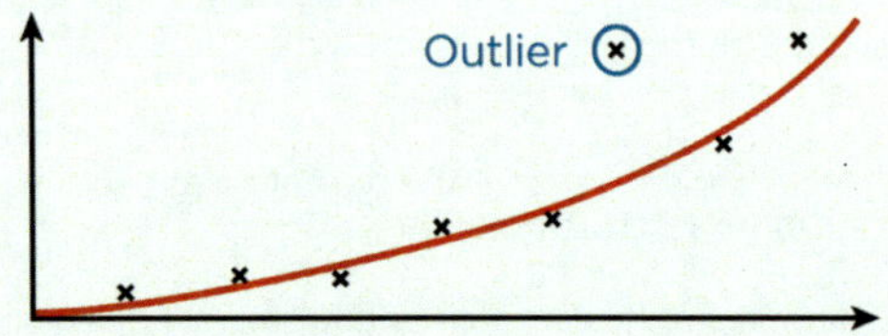

- Systematic errors are prevented through careful planning of experiments. This includes:
  - Ensuring all control variables remain unchanged during the experiment.
  - Calibrating all equipment and using it correctly.
  - Turning off equipment between measurements to prevent heating if temperature is a variable.
  - Testing equipment before an experiment.
  - Only measuring the meniscus at eye level when using a measuring cylinder.

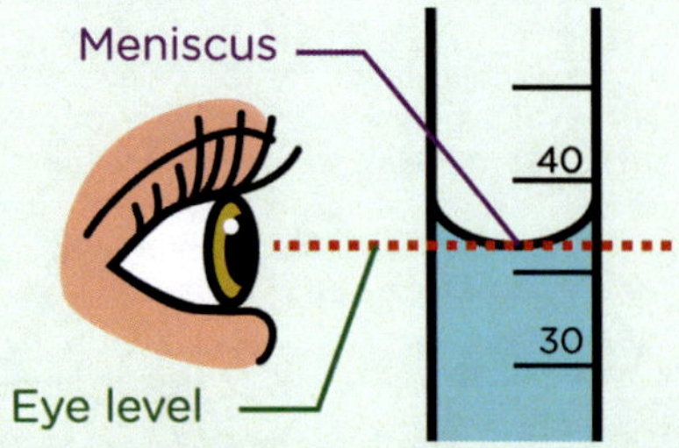

Units WS 4

- Measurements must be given units to indicate what they are measured in terms of.

Examples of units

Unit	Symbol	Quantity
Metre	m	Distance
Second	s	Time
Degrees Celsius	°C	Temperature
Litre	l	Volume
Grams	g	Mass
Joules	J	Energy
Coulombs	C	Charge

- Some units are derived as combinations of other units. For example:
  - Speed in metres per second, m/s.
  - Area in metres squared, m^2.
  - Rate in grams per second, g/s.
  - Density in kilograms per meter cubed, kg/m^3.

Prefixes WS 4

- Prefixes are added to units to indicate that they should be multiplied by a power of 10 to convert to the standard unit.
  - For example, $1\ cm = 1 \times 10^{-2}\ m$.
  - Prefixes are useful for writing out large or small values.
  - When substituting values into equations, their units must be converted to have the correct prefix first.

Prefix	Symbol	Multiplier
Tera-	T	10^{12}
Giga-	G	10^{9}
Mega-	M	10^{6}
Kilo-	k	10^{3}
centi-	c	10^{-2}
milli-	m	10^{-3}
micro-	μ	10^{-6}
nano-	n	10^{-9}